blueonblue

jordanparamor

CONTENDER
BOOKS

Interviews and text by **Jordan Paramor**

Blue is managed by **Daniel Glatman** for **Intelligent Music Management Ltd.**

First published 2002 by **Contender Books**

48 Margaret Street

London

W1W 8SE

www.contendergroup.com

This edition published **2002**

1 3 5 7 9 10 8 6 4 2

ISBN 1 84357 026 2

Design by **designsection**, Frome, Somerset

Repro by **Radstock Repro**, Midsomer Norton, Bath

Printed and bound in Great Britain by **Butler & Tanner Ltd**, Frome and London

Production: **Sasha Morton**

Contributor: **Michael Ibberson**

blueonblue

fame

A year and a half ago Blue were another undiscovered
act with huge ambitions, now they're the biggest pop band
in the country and get recognised everywhere they go.
So how are they handling fame and all that goes with it?
All will be revealed...

antony

'I still find it hard to
believe that I'm famous...'

I can have days when I walk down the street and I don't get recognised, then I'll walk down the street the next day and I get recognised everywhere I go. People are generally really cool with us, though. If I'm down the supermarket the lady at the checkout might ask for my autograph or something, and it's all part of the job. I like it. If people didn't recognise me it would be a problem so I don't mind at all. I get recognised at about 90 percent of the places I go to and I'm cool with it. I was out with my mates the other day and a lady came up to me and went, "You're that guy from Blue aren't you? Can I get your autograph for my daughter?" So I gave her an autograph and when she walked off one of my mates went, "That's so weird. We don't know you as Antony from Blue. You're just Antony to us." And that's it. I'm just me and I'm unaffected, and so are my mates. They don't tell any of their mates who I am or anything, and it doesn't mean a thing to them. That's the way I like it. They keep themselves to themselves.

The weirdest place I've been recognised is in the men's toilets in a club. I was having a wee and minding my own business, and when I went to wash my hands this geezer tapped me on the shoulder and I thought, "I'm in the toilets, there's no-one around, I'm gonna get beaten up here." And he said to me, "You're that bloke from Blue, right? I like your music son, you're alright." And I just went, "Thanks," and got out of there as quick as I could. You do get the odd guy who wants to have a fight because it's something to talk about with his mates in the pub the next day, but we pretty much get left alone. If I get hassled I try to take it on the chin, but I think we're pretty lucky in that quite a lot of blokes seem to like our music.

I think the whole fame thing really hit me when we won the BRIT Award. You can only win Best Newcomer once so that was wicked when we got it. It's the most prestigious award in Britain, and it was voted for by Radio One listeners and the fans, so thanks again to everyone that voted for us, and of course to Radio One for all their support. It was just wicked and I cried because I was so happy.

I don't think fame has changed me at all. I'm still the same Antony from Edgware. I'm a cheeky chappie. It's the people around me that have changed. People that used to speak to me don't speak to me any more. I'll call people and they'll talk to me for five minutes and won't know what to say, and then they'll say they have to go. But I don't know why they find it so hard to speak to me. I'm still me. I'm still the same person I've always been. I think people just don't know what to say to me at all. Apart from the boys I've only got about five brilliant, close mates that have always stuck by me. That's all I want. I get texts from people saying, "I haven't seen you for two years but can I get backstage passes for your concert?" It's madness. It's really not hard to spot that those people aren't trying to be your mate, they're trying to get something out of you.

The best thing about fame is that you get to go on really cool TV shows. You also get wicked free clothes. I got given a jacket once which was worth quite a bit. I wore it on a TV show and got to keep it so it's safely tucked up in my wardrobe now. Our stylist Caroline gets really good stuff for us and I always try to wind her up by nicking things. We got given a load of Timberland boots and Armani gear as well which was really cool.

We also get to be in magazines and travel the world. I'm only 21 and I've seen half the world already. People save up for years to go to Australia and I went last year, y'know. I'm so lucky. It's just a wicked job and I can't thank enough people that have helped me to get here: fans, my mum and dad, the record company, our manager, everyone that's believed in us. I think the worst thing about fame is that you miss your family and friends. It can be so tough because you can go for quite a while without seeing them, and I have times where I just want to go home and lie on the sofa and watch TV with my family. But you have to make sacrifices in this job and I understand that.

I think I've managed to keep my feet on the ground pretty well. You can't take it all too seriously. You can't let the whole fame thing go to your head and it's no good if you start to get complacent. I can understand why people go off the edge when they're famous because you're made to feel wicked. But the boys and me don't let it go to our heads. We won't let each other get out of control and become bigheaded because it would ruin things for the band. I never throw pop star strops, that's not me at all. I might have a little moan every now and again when I'm tired. I'll be like, "I look terrible, why do I have to do a photo shoot today? I look awful." But if people didn't want to take my picture I would worry, so I'm really aware of moaning as little as possible because I'm really incredibly lucky. We all are. The most showbiz thing I do is go to parties, but I don't do it to show off and hang out with celebrities, I do it to have a drink and laugh. We don't have limos or anything, I'm not into all that, it's not my scene. I'll get the 13 bus or whatever, I ain't bothered.

Sometimes when you're working really hard being in a band can be pretty tiring and you can feel pretty emotional. When I get like that I turn to my mum and dad, the boys, or my uncle. I've got a good support group around me, a really good family. My aunty Helen and her boyfriend Mike have always been really supportive and used to come to all the gigs I did before we made it. My mum and dad were the same, and my uncle George used to take me to gigs and look after me if blokes started on me or whatever. I'll never forget that. I'll never forget people that supported me and came and saw me before it all kicked off. My family are the people I trust and I know I can turn to anytime. I know they'll always be there for me. If I want to escape anytime I'll go to bed. I sleep as much as possible which tends to help because when you're tired things get to you a lot more. I also go to the local pub down the road. I know everyone and it's really laid back and it's a bit of a reality check for me.

Even when things have got tough, I've never wanted to give up on the band. I worked hard to get here and I'm not about to let it all go. Every day I look back to where I've come from and look at what I've got now and I can't believe it.

'I think the secret of Blue's success is that we've got a different sound, and our own unique look. We're just four normal boys doing what we love.'

duncan

'I think fame has been quite hard for me to accept because I'm just me doing what I've always done...'

I've always had quite a big group of mates and been quite popular, but not to the extent where every single person wants to know me and talk to me and watch me. I find it weird that I can't go into a pub now because people recognise you and you can feel their eyes on your back watching you. You're so conscious that everything you do is being watched. I find that really nerve-wracking and feel like it invades my space. There isn't a cut off point in this job. You can't go home from work and think, "I've finished for the day," and I think that's something you've got to accept. I'm finding it hard to accept that at the minute. I get recognised everywhere I go now. I'll be sitting on an aeroplane eating my meal and someone will come up to me. I was in Tesco's the other day and someone asked for my autograph. I'd only popped in for some bread or something! At first it was so cool to be recognised, and it still is, but sometimes I don't want to be spotted and I kind of hide. Sometimes I want to stay out of the limelight.

I can't do normal stuff now. I can't go out with my mates and get drunk and act stupidly because it would be a story in the papers the next day, or someone would be waiting for you to do something silly so they can tell everyone and put you down. I feel quite paranoid that people are going to sell stories about me. People think the whole fame thing is easy and it's all champagne and parties, but it's not. It can be quite lonely and you can become quite introverted and feel very isolated. You can be surrounded by so many people and still feel lonely. You constantly ask who your real friends are because it can be hard to tell. Everyone wants to know everything about you and you can't keep anything to yourself. I'm a good judge of character so I can tell who's just being mates with me because of the band. I'm quite a paranoid person and I worry about some of my friends. I worry that they think I've changed and that they're going to stab me in the back. I think a lot of friends can get jealous. They're like, "Oh look at him, he's doing really well and he's making money and he's just bought a new car." And they're pleased for you but they also think, "Why him? Why not me?" People can also be quite jealous because people want to talk about you and not them. That's really hard for people to handle and accept. And no matter how much they try not to let it bother them it does. I find that so hard and really upsetting because it's not like I want everyone to talk about me. It just happens that people are interested. Very often I'm like, "Don't ask me about my job, don't talk about me, I've finished work for the day now. Let's talk about someone else." But then if you don't want to talk about things people assume you're really rude and that you think you're great. It's hard to get the balance. But I sleep, eat and live this job and have been for the past year, and it's really hard to accept that everyone wants a piece of me. I need a bit of space sometimes.

The best thing about fame is being in the position that hundreds and thousands of people want to be in, and that's making music and performing. I never underestimate how lucky I am. Being on TV or making a music video are amazing things to do. I count myself so lucky every day that our album has been so successful and people like us. And I'm doing what I've always wanted to do. I keep myself down to earth by doing normal stuff I've always done, and I spend a lot of time with my mates. Hanging out with my mates and just being me is really important. I'd much rather do that than hang out at a showbiz party. We're not really showbizzy at all as a band. We don't really go out much and do all the parties. The most showbiz thing I do is drink champagne. I've got a taste for Kir Royals; that's my drink now. They give you bad hangover, though!

I've never had a full-on pop star strop, but we've all pulled a few little tantrums in our time when we've been away and haven't been told about stuff. When we went to the MTV Music Awards in Asia, it wasn't until we got out there that we were told we'd be performing and presenting an award, and we didn't have any clothes for it or anything, so we kicked off. And in Indonesia we were told we were doing a day of promotion with an artist out there, and when we got there we found out we were in her music video! It's things like that that drive us mad. It's lack of communication. We work so hard and if we don't know what we're supposed to do it's so hard. We're not puppets and we do have feelings so sometimes we do get upset. That's just normal and it's got nothing to do with us being in the band, it's just work stress.

I turn to my mum and my mates whenever I need support. But I wish my grandparents were still here because I would always turn to them if anything happened or when I needed help and support. I went to where I grew up the other day, to visit the old church that I went to, and lit some candles for my grandparents. Then I bought flowers and went to their graves and sat there and had a little cry. It was nice in a way. It's weird that they're not here anymore because they were always around, and this is the biggest change that's ever happened to me and I need them here. Sometimes I forget that they're not here, and for a split second I think I want to call my gran and then I remember that she's no longer there for me and it's horrible. I miss them so much.

'There's something for everyone in our band, and I think it really shows when we perform that we genuinely love it.'

There's never been a time when I've wanted to give up on Blue. There have been times when I've been like, "I can't handle this, I need a break and to get away." But I would never dream of leaving the band, I just mean I need to go away and sort my head out and come back fresh. I think that's when you realise you've got to dig deep, when it gets too much and you need to reassess. You need to draw on whatever you've got. We don't get a lot of time off so when we do it's precious. That's really your time to be normal again. Recently I escaped for the weekend to Bournemouth, but I even got hassled there. I was only in the hotel for two hours but it got passed round that I was there, and then next thing I knew all the staff and guests were coming up to me in the evening when I was having a drink with my mates. And I don't mind, but I'd gone away to get away from it all. I've learnt now that I just can't!

The best thing about being in Blue is the fact that we've been so successful. The album has sold over two million copies and has been number one in the charts, we've had number one singles, we've won a BRIT Award... I couldn't ask for a better year. We've been so incredibly lucky and everything has happened so fast. I look back and I think, "It was only a year or so ago that we were releasing All Rise and it was all kicking off." I remember thinking about it then and wondering where I'd be in a year's time, and here I am. It's incredible to look back and see what you have done. It's mad what we've done in a year. My sense of time is so warped now! I think the reasons things are going so well for us are good timing, good songs and good vocals. We were in the right time and right place with the right music and the right members. We all gel and get on so well, yet we're four different individual people who work really well together.

'There are always difficult aspects to every job, but I would never change what I'm doing right now. Being in Blue is amazing.'

lee

'Fame is a funny thing and I still can't see myself as famous...'

I'm not very good at playing the fame game. I'm still Lee from South London, and when I'm out and about people recognise me a lot now and it's so weird. It makes me laugh. I like seeing kids' faces when they see us. I remember when I was a kid and I used to meet famous people and I would get so excited. So I love it when kids get a kick out of meeting me. I would never think I'm superior because I'm famous, but if I can make a kid smile then that's brilliant. I'll always sign autographs for people, I'm more than happy to do that, but I don't really like it when I'm eating. Even then I'll still do it, but I would much rather people waited until I've finished eating.

I think fame has made me more wary of people and a bit less trusting that I used to be. Before I trusted anyone, but now I know the way people think and I know that some of them are trying to be friends with me for the wrong reasons. I can always pick up on when people are trying to be my mate because of Blue; you can see it in their eyes. But I guess I would probably be the same in their situation because I still get excited when I meet famous people. Some people try to be really low key when they meet us and pretend not to know who we are, but that's cool as well. If that's the way they want to be then fair play to them. We don't expect people to fall over backwards for us. My real mates spin out a lot because they still see me as little Lee who used to go out and party and get into fights. But my mates are still my mates. They're really protective of me, but there are still some places I can't go with them because sometimes people want to give me hassle because I'm in a band. I do have to be careful sometimes. Being in Blue is my job and I love singing, and when I first got into the band I thought it was all fun and games. And it is a lot of fun, but it's also a business and I've learnt that the most important thing is the singing. It's not about the parties or who you meet, it's all about singing for me. I learnt very quickly that I can happily do without the rest of it, but I can't do without singing.

I don't like the fakeness of the music industry, and the way the public perceive you. Things are said in the papers about us and the public get an impression of us which isn't always right. People don't know the real us but they think they do because they read things in the press. It's weird to me that people know so much about me but don't actually know me. But I know it comes with the job so I'm not complaining, it just does my head in when I think about it sometimes. We're never told what to say as a band and we're always ourselves. We've never been out to try and create a false impression of being this all-smiling pop band. We are what we are.

I think we've all managed to stay really down to earth and we haven't changed. I've never let everything run away with me. What's the point? I don't want to turn into a git. I do have strops sometimes, but that's not because I'm in a band and I think I can get away with it, it's just because I'm in a bad mood or whatever. It's really frustrating when everything is supposed to be really organised and things don't go according to plan. That's what drives me mad. It's a business, and if something's not right with my work I am gonna go mad about it. But I'm not going to turn around and throw a strop because someone hasn't put sugar in my tea or something. I just get angry for the normal everyday reasons that other people get angry.

There are some brilliant perks to being in a band. Being with the lads and having a giggle, and meeting all the people that are around us has been brilliant. We've got a really good team. We also get given some brilliant clothes. We're really lucky, and I give a lot of mine away to charity if I don't want them anymore. I give a lot of stuff to underprivileged families. I grew up in a one-parent family and my mum's worked hard for me. She did brilliantly at looking after me and giving me what I need, and now I want to help other people. Some people just need that extra little hand. I'm not fussed about money or materialistic things. It's nice to have nice things but it's not the end of the world if you don't have them. There are much more important things in life. I would never say I live a showbiz life, I don't like all that. None of us are really into the standing around at parties posing thing.

It sounds crazy but I probably have thought about giving up the band before. It's a mad, mad life doing what we're doing, but I know in my heart that I don't really want to give up. It just feels like it sometimes when I'm tired and I want to run away. But I know how good I've got it, and I know that I love my job. The feeling of wanting to get away never lasts long. I'm lucky because if I am stressed or upset, I can turn to my mum and my sister. My sister Jemma is 21 and we're really close. I call her Jem-bob and she's my skin and blister. I know they're always there for me and I can always call them if I'm away or talk to them when I'm home. We've always been close and they mean the world to me. If I'm stressed anytime we're away I'll go to my hotel room and chill out, or I'll take a bit of time out on my own. I like going on walks by myself; I can walk for miles. I remember when we were in Germany once and I really needed to get away from everything and have a think, so I went for a massive walk. It was raining but it was actually really nice because I could clear my head and give myself a good talking to.

'As for the future, we just want to keep on doing what we're doing. We're all having a laugh and like any job, there are pros and cons. But I can't complain. We're having the time of our lives.'

simon

'I don't think fame has affected me as a person one little bit...'

Being famous means that I can afford better clothes now, and I can go to the bank and get money out without checking my balance first, but it hasn't changed me from how I always was. It's probably made me a stronger person because I know I've got to learn to say "no" to people. People will take you for a ride whenever they can. I notice that when I go out I'm always the one buying the drinks, and I remember things like that. Even on my birthday people were coming up and saying, "Get me a drink." On MY birthday! The best thing about fame is that I get to do what I want to do with the boys. We're all doing what we love. The worst thing is that the tabloids want to know about your private life. Instead of concentrating on your music they want to slate you because you've got a daughter or your age is a year older than you say it is. That's what happened to me, and to me those things aren't a big deal but they're my private business. It's only when you're famous that things like that become a big deal to other people. I don't worry about stuff in the papers too much because tomorrow it's fish and chip wrap. I think being raised by my mother taught me what's right and wrong, and I know I'm a good person.

We get recognised all the time now. After All Rise was released we got recognised a bit, and we would look around to see if anyone noticed us. Then when Too Close went to number one more people recognised us and they started to ask us for autographs. Then If You Come Back exploded, and that was it, people knew us everywhere we went When we're out a lot of people say respect to us, and some people say they can't stand us, but you can't please everybody. It hurts when people say they don't like what we do because I want to know why, but it's their problem not mine I guess. I don't mind being recognised, although it's hard when I'm in a club with my mates having a drink and someone wants to take a photograph. I'm just trying to have a good time and people don't know that you're not working. I like to think I'm off duty when I'm with my mates, but really there's no such thing as off duty time. I've been in the middle of a dancefloor in a club and people have asked me for an autograph, so I've got to stop dancing and give them an autograph while standing in the middle of dancefloor in front of loads of people. It's hard not to look like you think you're really arrogant in that situation even though you're not, you're just trying to be nice.

A lot of my friends have been really supportive of me and the band, but I already kind of knew who my real friends were. A lot of people I know are more like associates, and they're just friends with me because of work and I know that. I'm not stupid, and I think sometimes people think I am. I'll let people take the p**s once, but they won't get away with it twice. And I am one to bear grudges. I remember what people do to me and I store it up and I use it. So if people cross me, they don't get away with it. I remember things that kids did to me in junior school and I still haven't forgiven them. I don't let people mess me around. It's funny how many people come out the woodwork once you get famous. All these people I was at school with that never talked to me now make out like we're good mates. They think I think I'm too good to talk to them, but that's not true. I just don't know who they are, they're not in my phone book, so why should I all of a sudden start acting like they're my mate?

My family are the ones that keep me down to earth. But then again, it's not about me needing it, it's about me being a good person anyway. I don't get above myself. I'm a naturally nice person, and I don't think you can fake being a nice person for long. You'll always be found out. My mum taught me that, she taught me the fundamental manners – hello, thank you, please, and goodbye – and that's all you need to get by. You can have all the money in the world, but if someone smiles and says hello to you and you can't say hello back, you ain't worth spit. I don't care how rich you are. I do get in bad moods from time to time and I may shout, but that's not me being a pop star, that's just me having a strop. I've never been like, "I can't work under these conditions, this room has to be blue." If I'm in a mood it's because I'm in a mood, not because I'm a pop star in a mood. But people see me and see a pop star in a mood and they judge, simple as that. But all I am is a guy getting a bit stressed. I don't get angry very often, and if I snap I apologise to the person I've snapped at straight away, then I forget about it. I get over it pretty quickly.

There are some times when I wake up and I wonder how I can make it through the day because I'm so tired. I'll wake up and think, "I can't do this today, I'm exhausted." But I always manage to get out of bed, and five minutes later I've been in the shower and I'm fine and it's all worth all the hard work again. It's just that going to bed at four and getting up at six for five days in a row is exhausting, and sometimes I feel like I can't handle it because I've got to go out and smile at everyone and be 'Simon from Blue'. But we grab kip wherever we can, and we always get through it. If I'm stressed or tired I'll turn to whoever's there. There's no-one in particular that I'll go to. I think we can all turn to each other. Sometimes a guy will be in a mood for a week, and you know that if they want to talk they will, and you give them space. We don't argue in the band. We have discussions if someone isn't pulling their weight or we want to change something, but we don't fall out. It's always a discussion and we're really honest with each other, which is why we work together so well.

The most showbiz thing I do is sing. I'm not interested in the showbiz parties; I'm not bothered. It used to be great and I loved them, but now it's hard to find a place where you can go out and people will be real. Everywhere we go there's always someone who wants to be an actor or a singer or a manager. You get guys walking round clubs saying to girls that look good that they should be a singer. They tell them that they're a manager, but they're talking rubbish. If anyone ever says that to you in a club, remember that you will never find an A&R man in a nightclub looking for talented people, you'll have a meeting with them in an office. So beware of what people will tell you. Another showbiz thing we do is get loads of clothes. We get given stuff by some really cool brands. Our stylist Caroline is the best and she always sorts me out with good clothes. I first met her at The Face of '98 model competition and she gave me a suit to wear. I was wearing this silky black and white shirt – which she said was disgusting – and she gave me this suit to wear instead, and I went on and won the competition. I'm still grateful to her for that.

The best thing about being in Blue so far is getting signed, and having number one singles and a number one album. And working with the boys every day. Everything is brilliant. I think the reason we're doing so well is because we're original. I have to admit I was scared of releasing All Rise because it was so different, but it was right for us and it worked.

'I think if we carry on the way we are then Blue can be around for a long time. If we keep putting out good music and the fans keep on giving us the wonderful support they have done then hopefully the future should look good for us.'

music

Money, fame and adoration are all part of being in a band, but for the members of Blue, the music will always be the most important thing..

antony

We've always said that music is what Blue are all about. We're a proper vocal group and we worked really hard to make an album which we could be really proud of. If You Come Back was the first song we ever recorded so that will always be special to me, and All Rise made us and brought us to where we are today. I also like This Temptation, which is one of the tracks we co-wrote, and Back Some Day is a really good song. My music tastes vary from anyone from Earth, Wind and Fire to Backstreet Boys and Westlife. I like all kinds of music. I've been brought up with Motown and soul and pop all my life.

Recording is a big part of our job, and I really like it, but sometimes it can get you down because you're in the studio and you're doing the same verse over and over again, and it's a head bang. I'll be like, "I don't want to do this anymore, I want to be in bed." But then you think, "Hold on, people would die to be here." So it spurs you on. Sometimes it gets you down, but I've really enjoyed working on the second album. It's been a slow process but it's been good. It hasn't been as intense as the first album because the workload has been broken up as we've been going abroad a lot promoting. It's been nice that it's broken up because I think I would crack up if we had to spend two solid weeks in the studio. We're really pleased with everything we've done so far and there will be a few surprises.

We had quite a big hand in the writing of our first album, which was brilliant. We co-wrote six tracks on there, and we've written a lot for the second album. It's important to me to write, but I also think that if a song is good we should record it. And if one of our songs isn't as good as a producer's is, we're not going to record it just because we've written it. We've worked with Gary Barlow, who used to be in Take That, on the second album. He's a great guy. I co-wrote with him and Elliott Kennedy and Tim Woodcock. The people I dream of working with are George Michael and Robbie Williams. They're my idols.

Making videos is a brilliant part of our job, I love it. It's a good crack because you get to have a laugh and hang out with all the extras. I really liked the If You Come Back video because there was a bit of acting in it, and Fly By was cool. But although I love the single All Rise, personally I don't like the video. I didn't feel good about it at all. I thought I looked terrible, although the other guys looked good. There's actually a dodgy bit in the video that no-one really knows about. If you watch me when we're doing the dancing bit where we're on a black floor I slip over at one point. There's a bit where you can actually see me slip, but unless you know it's there you won't see it, so keep a look out!

duncan

My favourite band are Travis, I think they're wicked. I think the melodies and everything are brilliant. I also like quite a lot of different music from the 70s, like funk and disco. Earth, Wind and Fire are a wicked band, and so are bands like The Temptations, and Motown bands. I'm also massively into Sheryl Crowe, she's fantastic, and The Stereophonics are great too. I think the 80s were a bit of a weird time musically, but I loved The Bangles and songs like Manic Monday and Eternal Flame. I really liked Oasis when they came out with the first album, and the same goes for Blur, but I was never massively into the whole Britpop scene. Out of all our songs, I think All Rise is the best. It's the song that broke us, and I'm still not bored of it even though we've played it hundreds of time. I'm proud of all our songs, though. I know a lot of people that are in bands and they don't like their own music and I think that's a real shame.

I love going into the studio to record tracks with the lads, you get to be creative and it's good fun. I don't like the waiting around that's involved with recording, but the rest of it I love. Producing really interests me generally and I'd love to get involved in that side of things. I'd like to work with The Neptunes, who produced the *N Sync track Girlfriend and Britney's Slave 4 U. They've got a really different sound. There's a real urban feel and they're edgy and sexy. I'd love for them to do one of our tracks one day.

We all do a lot of songwriting, but out of all of us I think Si does the most, and then Lee and then me and then Ant. If Lee's had a bad day or he's got something on his mind he can just write, Simon gets little melodies in his head and sings them, but I have to get inspired by something because I'm quite lazy sometimes. I'd rather just chill out with my mates than sit down and write songs. I can play the piano so I'll generally sit down at the piano at home and write. It's really important for us to be writing because it shows that we're not just another band that has songs written for us. It shows that we are creative and that we've got a brain and we can write songs as well as sing them.

We've written a lot for the second album and we're still working really hard on it. We want to have 30 tracks so we can pick 15 of the best like we did last time. We don't want to rush the album and get it done quickly; we want to take our time. We want it to be even better than the first album. I think the second album is when critics look at you and judge you, so we want to come back and say, "Bang! Look at that!" It's quite scary because people will be expecting a lot from us, but we listen back to the songs we've done for the second album so far and we're like, "Wow!" We're working with a lot of the same producers we worked with on the first album.

lee

I've loved music for as long as I can remember; it means everything to me. I'm into bands like 112, The Eagles, Mike and the Mechanics, Chicago, Toto and Jagged Edge. I like a lot of old school bands. I also like the music we do a lot, and I think Long Time is my favourite track on the All Rise album. There are some really good tracks on the second album as well. I think I'll enjoy the second album more than the first, maybe because it's new but I've got more experience now. I'm not nervous about what people think of it because even if it all ended tomorrow I'd still be proud and happy with what we've done. We've achieved so much already that if people like the second album as much as the first it will be a bonus. We've written nearly all of the second album ourselves, and I think we've done really well. Simon wrote a lot on the first album anyway because he did a lot of raps and stuff, but we all got really involved on the second album. Hopefully I'm going to have three tracks on the second album myself. I've been writing for years, and I love it. I always used to write poetry and stuff when I was at school, but I only really got into it properly when I was about 15. Funnily enough I never liked writing at school; I found it a bit boring. But when I left I started writing all the time and I really enjoy it.

I worked with Connor Reeves on a track for the new album. I think he's brilliant and when I was younger I used to sing his songs at karaoke nights down my way, so it was wicked to work with him. I'd also love to work with Brian McKnight. We met him recently and I was so terrified. Babyface would also be amazing to work with. But they're such experienced writers I don't think I'd be up to their standard, so I'd be really nervous. I'd want to get really involved but I wouldn't know what to say to them. If they turned round and said that something I did was wrong I wouldn't argue with them even if I didn't agree with them. It would be tough to talk back and you kind of need to do that when you're writing, so I'm not sure it would work that well.

Going into the recording studio is one of the things I love the most about this job. Being on stage is really cool, but when you're in the studio you can do your own thing. It's wicked. I enjoy making videos as well. We don't get to do it that often but we all really enjoy it. If You Come Back was my favourite video to make because I love the song. I love ballads.

simon

I love music and my favourite band at the moment are B2K. They're four guys from America and they're only about 15. They're bad. They're like a mini version of 112, and they're kind of Dru Hill-y. They've got nice voices and a nice sound. When it comes to our music my favourite tracks are Bounce, Long Time, All Rise, Fly By, Best In Me... the whole album, basically! It's so important to like your music. I was speaking to a band the other day and they were saying that they've changed their style of music recently and they like what they're doing, but they used to be really cheesy and they didn't like their music at all. I'd hate to not like my own music.

Recording is a really important part of the job and I love it. I love the idea of writing a song and getting it down in a studio. I love it when I write a song and I sing it to someone and they think it's kind of okay, and then when you put it down in the studio they're amazed by what you've done. I love going into the studio with nothing and coming out with something. The only thing I don't like about recording is when I can't hit notes. My voice is getting better and better but I can't stretch it as far as I'd like to yet.

We all do a lot of songwriting, and it's really important for us all to do it. I wrote quite a bit on the first album, which means a lot to me. I started writing songs when I was 15 when me and this girl called Lisa split up. My first song was called Why and it may be getting recorded now. It's weird because when I write songs I don't write them down, I store them in my head and write them down later. I wrote Why in my head on the bus, and then wrote it down later when I got home and kind of forgot about it, and now it may be a hit for someone. It's so weird. I enjoy writing for other people as well as the band, and I've got my own little label called Love For Music. I've also got another label called Flipside, which has got couple of remixes on it. I'm putting a band together as well, but all will be revealed about that in the future. It's all top secret at the moment.

The new album is coming along really well and we've worked with Stargate, Supaflys, Cutfather and Joe, and then individual people as well. Lee worked with Connor Reeves, Ant worked with Kenny Thomas, Dunk worked with Rob Davis who wrote Kylie's Can't get You Out Of My Head, and I worked with Ali Tennant and John Deeds. It's been brilliant doing the album. I am a bit nervous because people will expect a lot from us after All Rise, but I think they'll love this one as well. We've always been urban but with more of a pop influence, and this album is gonna be more urban. It's a bit of a move on, and it will be really good for America because we want to go to America with some hard stuff.

There are a lot of other musicians out there that I respect, and I would love to work with 112, Alicia Keys, Missy Elliott and Busta Rhymes one day. But even if I didn't work with them I'd like to able to speak to them on a one to one level, not as a fan. I met Busta Rhymes in Chinawhite once and I felt like a kid because I was watching all his movements and everything. I kept saying to myself, "What are you doing Si, you're in a band yourself so you know what it's like. Stop it!" At the end of the night I'd had a bit to drink and I went over and said thank you to him, but he didn't have a clue what I was saying thank you for. He just went, "Yeah, whatever dawg." I was actually saying thank you to him for inspiring me. He inspires me in the way he brings the screen alive and the way he performs, he's amazing.

We've enjoyed making all our videos so far, but I don't like it when we're separated from the other people that are in them. We like to hang out with the extras and have a laugh and chill. We're into being real and enjoying it, not having private rooms and being self-important. Too Close and Fly By were my favourite videos to make because we had really cool people there. All Rise is my favourite video because it was our first one, but that was just us four lads and I think we all agree that it's nice to have the extras there. And of course, we like having all the girls around!

a day
in their life

Every wondered what your favourite band get up to behind the scenes? We followed Blue around for a day to find out what life is like when you're in the biggest pop band in the country.

One word: Manic.

It's a grey, rainy day in London and at Heathrow airport in deepest West London the boys from Blue are preparing to touch down after a promotional visit to Sweden. Their schedule for today? A book signing in Bristol and then on to a concert called The Gig At The Gate which is being held at Bristol Football Club.

As soon as Blue land and make their way through the arrival gates fans descend upon them and ask for autographs. The lads happily sign everything from bits of paper to t-shirts before heading to their favourite airport hangout – the games room. Outside two Previas – huge family-sized cars which seat up to eight people – are waiting to zoom them to Bristol, and after 20 minutes playing on the arcade machines the lads are rounded up and herded into the first Previa alongside their tour manager, Johnny. The second Previa contains their hair stylist Liz, stylist Caroline (along with several cases and bags of clothes), a photographer, Francis, and another tour manager Sean who, along with Johnny, will be helping Duncan, Simon, Lee and Antony get from A to B throughout the day.

After heading off from Heathrow airport the first stop is a service station shop where the guys stock up on sandwiches, Pot Noodles, magazines, and in Duncan's case, a large bag of pick'n'mix. Once Lee gets his food he heads towards the CD section, which confuses Simon who thought Lee was making his Pot Noodle for him. "Nah man!" Lee laughs, "I'm too busy!" Everyone in the packed shop is trying to play it cool and pretend not to notice that Blue are wandering around, but they're obviously intrigued and keep nudging each other and giving the lads sideways glances. It's especially hard to ignore Simon, who is wearing a huge

hooded jacket and wandering around watching Under Siege on his beloved portable DVD player.

The lads spend the rest of the journey to Bristol catching up on their sleep, and two hours later The Big W store where this afternoon's signing is taking place comes into view. As the cars near the back entrance security gates are opened and after a quick check of the car, they're waved on through. Everyone is then led to a back room in the store where sandwiches, drinks, fruit, crisps and chocolate have been laid on for them. The lads mess around for a while and get their hair styled by Liz, then it's off to another room where around 30 competition winners are waiting nervously to meet the band. The lads pose for photos, sign autographs and kiss the excited fans, then it's time to face the 2,000 strong crowd which have gathered outside. An area contained by wire fencing has been sectioned off for the signing, and numerous security guards surround a table which has been set up for the guys to sit at to greet all the fans. The queue is enormous, and ages range from toddlers to grannies. The second Blue appear everyone starts screaming, and the lads give them all a wave. All Rise blasts out of a huge stereo and Lee demands that the crowd, "Scream louder!" before the guys take their seats and prepare to get signing. As well as the fans, some of the lads' families have turned up to see the signing, and Antony's mum, dad, sister and brother watch alongside Duncan's mum, who has come

along specially to take photos for the Blue fan club newsletter.

An hour and a half later a zillion autographs have been signed and many excited tears have been shed, and it's time to head to the venue for this evening's gig. As Blue leave The Big W store fans chase the cars down the road shouting and waving furiously as Lee and Duncan stick their heads out of their car's sunroof and blow kisses.

The lads are headlining tonight's gig where they will be performing alongside other chart acts, and they can't wait. "Performing is our favourite thing to do," says Ant, "it's what it's all about." As soon as they arrive the guys are led to their dressing room, which boasts an impressive array of drinks – vodka, coke, beer, orange juice, apple juice, tons of water, and the rock stars essential, Jack Daniels! But it's the water that's most important to them and they sip hot water throughout the run up to their performance to clear their throats and enable them to sing better.

Just down the hall from the dressing room is the artist catering room where all the acts hang out and chat before and after they go on stage. The food on offer includes chicken curry, pasta salad, fruit cocktail and chocolate brownies – which go down a treat with all the artists. Dunk, however, has other ideas about dinner, and disappears for half an hour before coming back into the dressing room rubbing his stomach. "I've been in the directors' box eating salmon, prawns and profiteroles," he explains, "I feel sick now!" There are a couple of hours before they have to be on stage, and as well as hanging out in artist catering, the guys pass the time by doing impressions of Ant (Dunk) and Lee (all of them). They also have a few friends and family back for a drink and a chat, including Ant's best mate from home, George. There's still a bit of time left before the gig so Simon watches another DVD, Lee pops off to artist catering, and Dunk and Ant are given a facial by Liz. Then it's time to decide what to wear and one at a time they go through the rails of clothes with Caroline and select the outfits they'll be performing in.

Shortly before they're due on stage everyone is asked to leave the band alone in the dressing room so they can go through a warm-up with their voice coach, Stevie.

And 20 minutes later – after a short pep talk from Johnny during which they're told in no uncertain terms to make sure they pick up the right earpieces – the lads are ready to work their magic. Despite the fact that it's pouring with rain outside, thousands of fans are waiting patiently for the guys to take to the stage. They wave banners and chant "Blue" in anticipation, then suddenly they surge forward as the stage lights are dipped and dry ice begins pouring out from the back of the stage. Blue's band and two female backing singers are first to take their places, and a minute later Blue run on and stand in front of their mikes, heads bowed. The crowd roar and the stage trembles with the sheer volume of the music as Dunk, Lee, Simon and Ant break into Too Close. Dunk air guitars with the bass player, Ant runs madly from one side of the stage to the other, and Simon flings an arm around Lee as they belt out the number one track. Next comes Fly By and the crowd sing along as the lads go mad, clearly having the time of their lives. Their beautiful ballad Long Time is next, followed by a cover of The Temptations' classic Get Ready. If You Come Back gets an incredible reception, as does This Temptation. Best In Me goes down a treat, and the crowd go wild when All Rise makes an appearance for the encore.

Backstage afterwards the lads are elated – it's gone well. They talk about where they could improve things next time, and the best bits of the show, but ultimately decide that the night was a big success. They are soon changed back into the clothes they were wearing earlier in the day, and all admit that they're looking forward to heading home for a good sleep. As they jump into the Previas and drive out of the venue, once again fans run after the car. The lads give a final wave as their cars speed off in the direction of London, and then it's all over for another day. Now there's just tomorrow to think about...

around the world

Travelling goes hand in hand with being a pop star.
The lads fill us in on lost luggage, huge phone bills,
drinking snake's blood, and Lee's pant borrowing habit...

We've visited so many places now, and I have to say I think the country I enjoyed the most was Australia. It's so far away, but it's got such wicked people and it's a gorgeous place. I think the cold countries are probably my least favourite places to visit because when you go from England where it's always cold to another European country where the weather's the same it's a bit depressing. When it comes to being offered weird food and stuff, I haven't really come across much because if something looks weird, I won't eat it – unlike Lee who will try pretty much anything. We get given amazing presents when we travel and in Thailand and Taiwan and Indonesia and places like that the girls give you amazing things. They give you beads, chains, books on their culture and models of things; really nice stuff that you can't get over here.

antony

It takes me about half an hour to pack to go away. I've got it down to quite a fine art now, but I always take more clothes than I need. And then come back with more than I went with because I'll have been shopping. I always make sure I pack simple clothes like jeans because they're easy to bung on, and I always take my phone and my DVD player because they go everywhere with me. I probably take the most luggage out of all us because I always take extra stuff just in case, whereas Lee always forgets everything. He's terrible. He's always like, "Ant, can I borrow a top please bro, I didn't know we needed to bring lots of stuff." Then you don't see it for the next six months.

I really miss my family and my mates when I'm away, big time, and if I'm away my phone bills are massive.

Of the countries we've been to so far I loved Australia, New Zealand and Singapore. South-East Asia in general is quite hard to visit because not only are you working really hard, but also you're battling against the heat and you can't drink the water. And it's so far away that when we go there, we go for a good couple of weeks and I can get depressed and miss home. Friends, family and my bed are the things I miss most when I'm away. I'm on the phone a lot and my bills are huge. But more worrying than the bills, I think about how badly my brain's been fried!

We haven't had any really terrible journeys so far thankfully, but we have done a lot of travelling and we've had some hectic days. Some days we've done a whole day's work and driven from Manchester to Devon, then done a gig in London, then driven to somewhere like Nottingham. We've figured out that we've worked 23-hour days before.

duncan

We do have a fantastic time being away though. Sometimes we get really sweet things happening to us, like when we went to Malaysia and Singapore we got to the hotel and all the staff greeted us by standing in a line with a red carpet. And they bow at you and put these orchids around you and worship you. It's a bit odd, but it's lovely.

And when we were in Taiwan we all had our own butlers, which was so weird because they wait on you hand and foot. We totally weren't used to it. Some fans in other countries are pretty crazy, especially in places like Indonesia and Bangkok. They don't get to see many Western acts, and they're not like kids over here, they're very different. They're lovely, they look about 14 but they're usually about 21. We've been given lovely presents all around the world. The fans have been so amazing. For instance, I take my pillow everywhere with me – I'm a big baby like that and I need my sleep. I can't stand it when you get on planes and get that tiny little pillow. Anyway, there are a couple of fans we know called Tammy and Jenna and they're really nice girls, and they had a pillow case specially made for me with two big boobs on it. And underneath one it says 'Tammy' and underneath the other one if says 'Jenna'. They say that now when I sleep I can have my head in between their boobs! It's funny things like that that I love. I also get little teddy bears and ornaments and stuff, and books that fans make. One girl made a cross-stitch picture of me and it was so clever. I get some beautiful stuff.

It doesn't take me long to pack when we're going travelling, I just chuck everything in my case. I never iron my stuff; I iron when I arrive at places. I think we all take about the same amount of stuff beforehand. We sort of know now how much we need. I tend to fold my stuff quite well so I can get it in. Lee's stuff is always kind of chucked into his case, it's picked up off the floor and thrown in. Because of that he always forgets his underwear, like his socks and pants. He's always like, "Dunk, can I borrow some underwear or socks." And I end up having to go out and buy more. I don't think he'll ever remember them.

We've been so lucky being in Blue because we've got to visit some incredible places that we probably would never have been to otherwise. For instance, some places in Thailand are just mad and their culture is amazing, so it's brilliant to see all that. I think my favourite place we've been to is Australia. It's really cool and the people are brilliant. Asia is also amazing but can be quite full-on. As soon as you land they stick cameras in your face which can be scary. And they eat some weird food, but I don't mind that at all. I'm intrigued and I don't mind trying stuff. I'll eat anything. I can't remember where we were but this one time we were offered the chance to drink snake's blood. It's a spiritual thing that's meant to bring you luck. They cut the snake and you drink the blood while the snake is still alive. I would have done it but we didn't have time. Duncan was horrified, he said there was no way he would do it. But I was well up for it.

Fans are the same wherever you go, they're brilliant and really supportive. They're pretty full-on in Taiwan. When they start screaming in my face I scream back at them and they scream even louder!

It's mad. I've had to tell a couple of people over there to get off me before because they've hurt me. I think sometimes people forget that we're human and that it hurts when they grab you. We get given nice presents wherever we go. I like it most when we get given poetry. I read a lot of the letters and stuff we get, and it's nice that someone has taken the time to sit down and write something. I think it's good for kids to write poetry because I don't think they get enough chance to be creative at school. They're just told to copy things out of a book. So I really like it when I get creative stuff from our fans. It means a lot.

I'm a terrible packer when we go away. If I'm at home I'll just chuck anything in, and then when I get to places I realise I've got nothing to wear. I take a lot of stuff with me but none of it is any good once I get there. I don't know how I have so much stuff but never have what I need. It's a mystery. The things I always forget are socks, pants and my toothbrush, so I have to buy or borrow them. I've got so many toothbrushes now. I don't know why I never remember them, you'd think I would after forgetting them so many times. I can survive with very few clothes though, I've learnt to do it. I remember this one time my luggage didn't get delivered so I had to go out and buy some more clothes. I was wearing a pair of jeans, and I can live in a pair of jeans for a week so all I needed to get was a couple of t-shirts and I was sorted. I never fold anything when I pack, I just shove it in. That's why it takes me about ten minutes to do the lot. Packing to me is boring so I don't really bother too much. I just get it out of the way quickly. Ant is always really organised and everything is always packed perfectly, and wherever we are he always has everything laid out neatly the night before. I just wake up and grab whatever. I'm always in a rush and I don't think that's ever going to change.

I really miss my mum and my sister and my mates when I'm away, which is why my phone bills are so big. I've been trying to calm down lately, but I have had ridiculously huge phone bills in the past. That's just mad. I've got to calm it down!

I reckon the best places we've visited so far would be Sydney, Singapore and Thailand. I love Asia full stop, and I love the Asian people. They make you feel so welcome. We always get a great welcome wherever we go, but some places make you feel so special and treat you so well, and in Asia they're always so glad to see you. They're quite full-on, but lovely. Asia has got some quite strict customs, and when we went there we were told that we couldn't wear blue jeans or show off our tattoos because it's a Muslim country. It's their culture, and you've got to respect that. I even wore a sarong in Asia! A fan gave it to me and I wo re it that night. Everyone was laughing at me and calling me Simone, but I didn't care. I was getting in with the culture, man.

Fans are great in other countries, they're just as good as they are in the UK. They go out and buy our music and they're really supportive, and that's what it's all about – the music. The fans do try and get a piece of you in Asia, though. They grab at you because they're just so happy to see you, and they can end up taking chunks out of you. The fans give us such amazing presents over there. They fold up these really tiny stars by hand and give them to you in a jar. You get about 99 in a jar, and it's so special because it takes a lot of effort. Some of them draw portraits of us and make us into Manga cartoons and stuff, which is very cool. I've got them all at home, and I've also got a doll of me which one fan made which is wicked.

We've been really lucky with our travelling and haven't had too many nightmares. You get your odd delay here and there, but somehow we always manage to swindle getting onto the next plane. We hear people standing around saying they've got to wait for two days for a flight, but we generally get on the next plane. We're really, really lucky.

simon

My suitcase is always packed ready to go away at all times. I've got a suitcase I use for travelling, and then my clothes that I wear all the time, so as soon as I get back from abroad I wash everything and it goes back into my case so I'm always ready. Lee, on the other hand, is never ready and always forgets things. He borrows everyone's stuff and I can't understand why he never remembers anything! I take so much with me when we go away, I'm always well equipped. As well as my clothes I have to have my DVD player, DVDs, Clinique toiletries, and my phone. It's mad but because I'm always calling home my phone bills are massive. But it's worth it to stay in touch with my family and friends.

before they were famous

All the Blue boys knew from an early age that they wanted to perform, but the road to fame isn't always a smooth one and troubled school days, dodgy jobs and bad advice were all a part of Blue's rise to the top...

antony

I knew from when I was really young that I wanted to be a singer or an entertainer. I used to do stand up comedy when I was younger, but it was such a hard job, but I still loved it because I loved any kind of performing. I did a show once when I was 13 and I made people laugh so I was alright. But if people don't laugh at you it's the worst thing in the world. I didn't go to drama school as a kid, I didn't want to, but I used to go to drama classes at Sharon Harris in Wembley every Thursday evening, and I loved that. It taught me a lot and I always really looked forward to going. I loved putting on the shows and everything.

Job wise, I did a few acting jobs when I was younger. I was in The Bill, Chalk and Grange Hill, and if I wasn't in Blue I think I'd still be acting. That's how I started and I still love it. I used to do a lot of bar work as well, and I used to help my dad with car-boot markets to get some extra money. I also used to help out my uncle George because he was in the women's fashion game. My uncle George is like a second brother to me, we're really, really close. Sometimes if I can't talk to my parents about things – which isn't very often to be honest – I'll talk to my uncle and he'll give me advice. He's always been there for me.

'We got a record deal and things really took off... we haven't looked back since.'

My drama teacher at school, Mr. Jones, gave me the chance to star in one of his musicals when I was only 14. I was one of the youngest cast members to have a main part in the show Cabaret, which was brilliant experience for me. I remember at school my teachers all used to say to me, "Look Ant, you'll never be a singer, get yourself a proper job." They just used to tell how one in nine people make is as a singer, etc, etc. But when they saw me in Cabaret they held their hands up and admitted they'd made a mistake and that I should pursue it. That felt pretty good. I would like to go back and say to them, "Look, I did alright." I'd like to take my BRIT Award along to show them all! I think teachers should encourage kids more where singing and performing is concerned. That's why England isn't very good at sports, because kids are never allowed to pursue it.

The best job I did when I was younger was obviously acting, but the worst was tele-sales. I found that so degrading. It was really embarrassing and I used to get paid by the month so I'd be skint for three weeks because I'd blow all my money in the first week. I'd end up having to live on £50 a week, which was a nightmare. Directly before Blue started I was doing bar work and auditioning for things. That's where I met Dunk, on the audition circuit. We met about three years ago when I was 18. We were both in bands already but we decided to form Blue. Then we got Lee and Si in, and at first it was a bit of a hobby because we didn't have any money or anything. But then we got a record deal and things really took off. Obviously we haven't looked back since. It's been mad, but amazing. When I was at school my careers advisor told me that I should be a travel agent or a funeral director. I've got no idea how he came to that conclusion, but he couldn't have been more wrong!

duncan

My first-ever job was working in a hotel in Sidmouth on a Saturday when I was 15 years old. My mum owned a caravan site in Sidmouth and she used to let me work in the shop that was attached to it and I used to check people in. We had a quad bike so in the summer it was my job to drive people to their pitch. That was great. Just over the road from the caravan site was a golf range, so I also had a job there where I would drive around this quad bike which had a net across the back that picked up all the golf balls

that much money. When we lived in Devon her boyfriend had a nice house and everything, but I still always worked so I had my own money. Even if your parents are stinking rich, I don't think you should rely on them. It's important to be independent. My worst job ever has to be when I worked in Harvey Nichols, Selfridges and Harrods spraying people with aftershave. It was so demoralising and people were so rude. There was me wanting to be an actor or a singer or something, and instead I was stuck

'When Blue came along I knew straight away it was right, it was everything I wanted in a band.'

as you drove over them. Of course people would whack the balls at me and try and hit me, but luckily I was in a little cage! I also worked in Woolworth's and in a café, and I was an usher in a cinema in Sidmouth. At ice-cream time I would stand up the front of the cinema in my suit and bow tie with a torch and sell ice creams. It was a proper old-fashioned cinema where I'd get to watch all the latest films and my mates would come along and watch them too. When I first moved to London I worked as a waiter in an American food chain. I could earn £40 a night in tips, which was fantastic. I've also done pub work, been a barman... Just about every job going!

I was lucky as I didn't have too many bad jobs, although I did once work in a supermarket as a checkout operator for four hours a night and some Saturdays. That wasn't that much fun. After that I'd go and work in the cinema in the evening, then sometimes I'd go in on a Sunday too because you got double pay. I've always worked really hard because being a single parent my mum never had

with all these pretentious people who were rude to me. I had to stand there for eight hours a day and wasn't allowed to sit down. They only paid me £50 a day and needless to say I didn't last that long. I hated it.

I always wanted to be an actor when I was at school. I was lucky enough to go to a school where we had a really good drama department. Miss Davis was the head of the drama department and she also used to run the Youth Theatre which would put on major productions in the Manor Pavilion in Sidmouth. It was quite a major thing and she was an amazing drama teacher. I was also in the Sidmouth Amateur Dramatic Society. I remember when we did the open-air production of Midsummer Night's Dream for the International Folk Festival in Sidmouth and I played Puck. Every year people came from all over the world to take part in it. I was lucky because I was very close to Miss Davis and she would give me great parts, usually the singing ones, and a lot of leads. I think if I wasn't in Blue I would be acting.

I would love to be in the theatre in the West End. The careers advisors told me that wanting to be an actor was a rubbish idea and one said she thought I should go into public relations because I was good at talking to people. She got that right, but she was way off with the job!

Just before Blue I was in another band called Tantrum with Rita from Girls @ Play, Zac from Northern Line, a girl called

April May, and Jonus Hearst who's now doing presenting work. We had fun and it was a great experience for me to learn about recording studios and all about making an album. It also enabled me to realise what I wanted to do and to make great friends. Rita is one of my closest friends now, I love her to bits. She's a great girl, so a lot of good things came out of it. When Blue came long I knew straight away it was right, it was everything I wanted in a band. It's so perfect for me and I wouldn't change it for anything.

lee

I wanted to be a singer from the age of eight. I just loved singing and I wasn't very good at anything else. When I was young I used to watch a lot of people like Michael Jackson, Boys II Men, Lionel Ritchie, Diana Ross and Elton John – people with really big voices. I wanted to be like them. I wasn't very good when I was in school and I never wanted to wear school uniform. I especially hated wearing my tie so I was always getting into trouble for taking if off. I used to mess around a lot as well. I remember this one time when my teacher went out of the room for two minutes, and when she came back in I was hanging from the bars on the ceiling pretending to be a monkey. Not surprisingly she chucked me straight out of the class, and that was the first of many times.

When I went to drama school it was pretty much the same except I was dancing and singing. But I did calm down a lot when I was there. I think it was because I was able to sing all the time. Also, when I was at drama school my teachers encouraged me because they all seriously thought I could do drama or singing as a career. That made me behave a bit better.

As soon as I was old enough to work, I did. I did everything: worked on a building site, in a hairdresser's, in cafés, I did cleaning... You name it, I've probably done it. I always worked after school to get money. Always. I didn't really have any bad jobs though, because I thought any job that gave me money was cool. My mum always said to me that no job is a bad one, and I agree. Anything that earns you dough is good. It's up to me whether or not I enjoy a job, but I'm always thankful to have one. If I lost this job tomorrow I'd go and get another one and I wouldn't mind what I did. I'd really miss being in Blue and I'd miss the lads a lot, but I'd know that I had to work so I wouldn't think twice about starting work again straight away. This job is without a doubt my best job; it's everything I've ever wanted to do. I was always determined to do something in the entertainment industry and then Blue came along. And if I hadn't joined Blue? I'd still be trying to make it as a singer. I would never have given up.

'If I hadn't joined Blue? I'd still be trying to make it as a singer. I would never have given up.'

simon

The first job I ever had was breaking down boxes in a fruit and veg shop. It was great because I was working with these girls called Claire, Joanne and Sarah and they used to beat me up. Only in a friendly way, though! I was there for about a year and it was a good laugh. I also used to work for the council and sweep the Bullring Market in Birmingham four days a week after school. The worst job I've ever had was working in a fridge stacking milk. It was eight degrees and I used to stand in there for eight hours at a time. I used to be freezing and stinking of milk. It got to the point where I hated the smell and even the sight of milk.

had music inside me trying to get out and I used to ignore it. Now we've not only got a million-selling album, but I've got five tracks on there that I've co-written, and I can't believe it. It's such an incredible feeling. Even back in my early schooldays I wanted to be a footballer or a superstar. I remember when Michael Jackson's BAD album came out, and there was this huge billboard with him lying down on it. I was only about ten but I looked at it and three things went through my mind – modelling, football and singing. And I've done all three. In fact, in this job I get to do all three. I get to play in the Soccer

> ### 'We always knew we'd get here, and signing on the dotted line when we got our contract was the best feeling.'

I also did modelling for a while because I won a Face of '98 model competition. It was such a surprise because I'd never modelled in my life and they chose me out of the whole of England. I was so lucky. But modelling isn't all it's made out to be. It's a bit degrading. I say that because I didn't get much work at times, and when you're a model and you're not getting work there's nothing worse. If you haven't got 'the look' of the moment, forget it. After a while it starts to hit home that you're not getting work because you don't look right, which doesn't make you feel good. I don't miss modelling at all. I was glad to be out of it. My best job has to be getting into Blue. I couldn't get a job better than this. It's just amazing. I think I was born to do this. Even as a kid I knew I would be doing it. I did think for a while that I would become a footballer, but I got injured and that put paid to that. But I've never regretted what happened. I think life has its own path and if I'd carried on with the football I wouldn't be doing this now. All my life I've

Six competitions, model in magazines and I get to sing. It's such an amazing job. I was pretty well behaved in school, and if I was to write a report on myself I would say: "Simon has the ability to learn and is very easily distracted, but is a good boy." I never had the best trainers or anything when I was growing up, but I was always brought up well. I was polite to the teachers and was headboy at my school.

If I wasn't in Blue I would definitely be in the entertainment business doing something. That's why I was doing modelling – to try and get my foot in the door. I went for parts in Hollyoaks and stuff, but I didn't get them. And because I didn't get them I knew that something better would come along, and here it is. Directly before Blue I was working in Lee's mum's hairdressing shop washing hair. I worked there for about two or three months until we got signed. The waiting in

between us getting together and getting signed was horrible. We kept thinking we would get a deal and then it wouldn't happen, which was so frustrating. The thing is you get used to being disappointed, so when something does happen you appreciate it and it was worth the wait. We always knew we'd get here, and signing on the dotted line when we got our contract was the best feeling. We didn't know what we were signing but we didn't care because we were too excited. And the gamble certainly paid off.

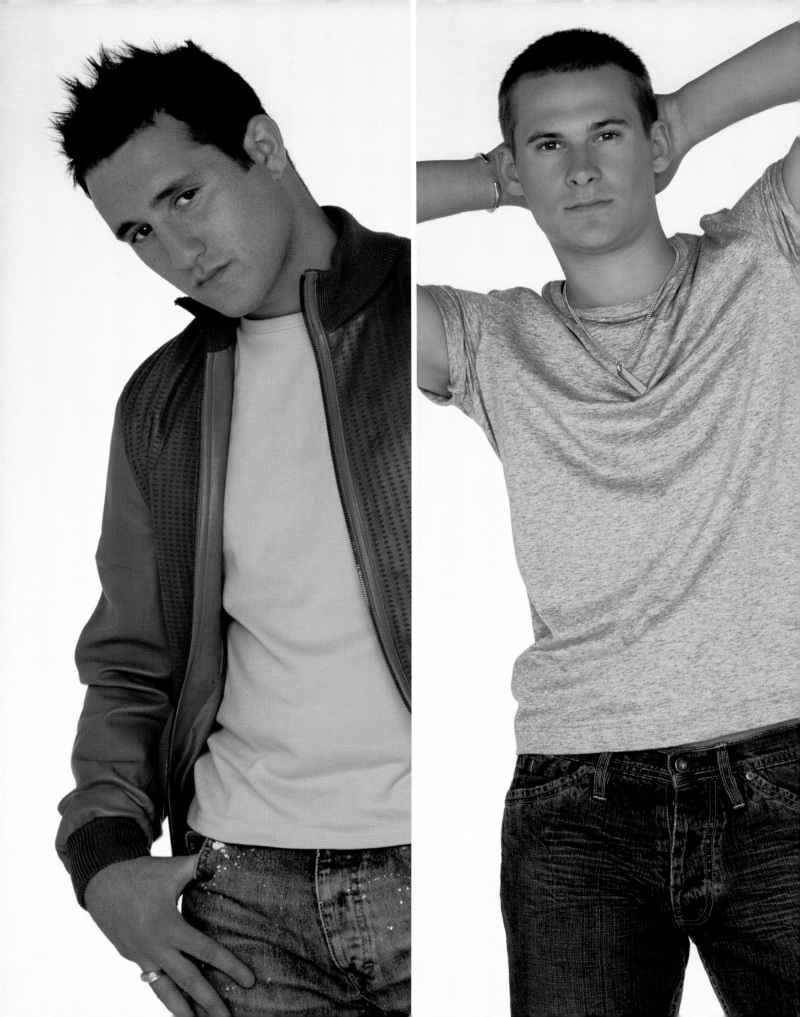

...ny in Co...
...s well as in Sw...
...character...ations Sub-standard...
...because...Sub-standard...
...nes... and I believe he has...
...self down... by his behave...
...to let but all too often...
...needs... to Sir david and...
...esire to became a profess...
requires - hard work, dev...
...xtermination - without pla...
...natural ability becomes pla...
...dard... ...ng and hard!

...enjoyed... throughout the...
...ked well... result was disappointing...
...'s work.
...term's work, followed... result...
...pleasing... exciting result...
...puts... himself complet...
...work. Well done. B.
...' work is stronger th...
...tten work and his...
...reason is still tremend...

English:
...Antony has a...
...ng: spoken English and is...
...communicating his thoughts...
...listen a little more. He seems...
...of books... reading and has read a number...
...books, a book of cats etc...
...writing is maturing, and the content is sta...

MATHEMATICS Antony enjoys maths and is...
...en to try more challenging / difficult...
...work. He sometimes gets a bit disap...
...his strength is that he is alw...
...to try again.

...enjoys science...
...it is very...

Technolog...
...design... he can...
...processing tasks.
...amming progra...
begun to do well...
...hard... think this...
...well... overall...

...continued to progress stea...
...achieved a great deal...
...all miss his cheerful smi...
...little voice. I know th...
...Lives? at a middle School and...
...very happiness and success...

...and...
...humble member...
...popular gentleman...

Days Absent: 1.

Headmaster's Report

...Duncan puts a...
...am sure he will do well...
...hope to hear lots of...

...achieve... with accurate, qui...
Good work also in measures usi...
Improving skills at using / applying ma...
also problem solving / investigational work.

...good cum...
He is a well-mann...
boy who is reliable and help...

Attendance: V.Good.
Signed A.Waugh (Class teacher) **Date** 17:06:9...
...TON EDUCATION

SCIENCE
...his science work. He can...
...able level

The Italia Conti Academy
of Theatre Arts Ltd

LEE RYAN

Report

English -
...hindered by absence.
...progress with his reading but...
He has a very active imagination which he puts to
full use when writing stories. The ideas he puts
forward in discussion are after the starting point
for the rest of the class.

ths - Simon is slow to complete his written maths but always
gets there in the end. He enjoys practical activities
and can be relied upon to work on his own without
supervision.

al - He has made steady progress in all...
at all sports...

...mbled bit of paper
...ped up and savag...
...always mor...
...when you were ha...
...re sad, please tell...
...things...
...turn out so...
...pain was also hard...
...believe...
...d you up and ch...
...sold all your...
...tell me why you...
...why you stayed?/...

...early keen to...
...himself on. Howev...
...e sometimes tries...
...ase both adults...
...erms of his work...
...the quality...

...Standard and...
...how did ...
...Duncan...
...please...
...reading ...

school

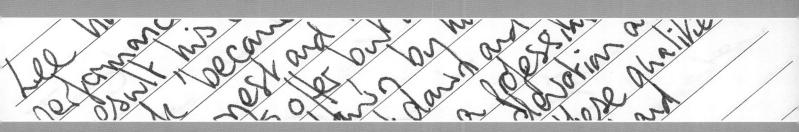

We got hold of some of Blue's old reports to find out what
they were really like at school.

It seems that Antony was very popular, often cheeky, and loved reading his, er, 'Book Of Cats'...

Annual Report for Parents 1991

School *Ambler Primary School*

Name *Antony Costa*   Date of Birth *26·6·81*

LANGUAGE Greek / English.

Speaking & Listening: Antony has a very good command of spoken English and is very good at communicating his thoughts. He needs **Reading:** to listen a little more. He seems to enjoy reading and has read a number **Writing:** of books A book of Cats etc. His handwriting is maturing, and the content is starting to reflect his wider reading.

MATHEMATICS Antony enjoys maths and is keen to try more challenging / difficult work. He sometimes gets a bit disappointed, but his strength is that he is always prepared to try again.

SCIENCE Antony enjoys Science and finds the Science activities very stimulating. He is excited to get the right conclusions, gradually getting better at using information, recording and predicting.

(E98)

Other aspects of learning and development

Antony has been at the school for four months, he has settled down and made a number of friends.

He is clearly keen to do well and pushes himself on. However, I feel that he sometimes tries too hard to please both adults and his peers. In terms of his work he needs to concentrate on the quality, and not rush his work just to get something in. Recently he has been acting a little silly in order to be accepted, he has a lot of good qualities, like keenness and a willingness to work, he should build on these qualities and have a little more confidence in himself and I think he should go far.

Signed   Class teacher *J. Bunbury*

Head teacher *A. Gordon*   Date *7/91*

ISLINGTON EDUCATION

Annual Report for Parents 1992

School *AMBLER*

Name *ANTONY COSTA*   Date of Birth *23:06:81*

LANGUAGE

Speaking & Listening: A confident and enthusiastic speaker. Speaks clearly & fluently; contributes usefully to discussions. Good listening skills and quick to pick up new ideas.

Reading: An enthusiastic, fluent, accurate & very expressive reader with good comprehension and retention.

Writing: Antony writes quickly, neatly, and well with good grammar, spelling and punctuation. Good creative ideas. Sometimes gets factual writing muddled.

MATHEMATICS Antony enjoys his maths and has made very good progress this year. He has achieved a high standard in his arithmetic with accurate, quick recall of times tables. Good work also in measures and geometry. Improving skills at using/applying maths as also problem solving/investigational work.

SCIENCE He enjoys his science work. He can hypothesise at a reasonable level and is beginning to be able to draw generalised conclusions.

TECHNOLOGY; including Information Technology
With a little guidance he can plan and execute simple design tasks. Can use a simple word-processing program; good graphics work; beginning to use data base well.

OTHER ASPECTS OF LEARNING AND DEVELOPMENT
Antony is keen to do well and he has worked hard this year. Sometimes he needs to think a little more carefully and deeply about his work as he often lets his enthusiasm run away with him.
He has also developed an understanding and knowledge of history and geography, particularly map skills. He has improved the quality of his art work. Good progress on guitar. Antony is very able physically, a popular member of a team. Also a good canoeist and can swim 400m. He is a well-mannered, polite, friendly boy who is reliable and helpful.

Attendance: V. Good.

Signed *A. Waugh (Class teacher)* Date *17.06.92.*

A. Gordon

ISLINGTON EDUCATION

Your teachers seemed to like you. Did you get on well with them?

There were a few that I did get on with and a few that I didn't. I think the ones I didn't get on with I was pretty false with. I used to get on with my drama teacher really well, Mr.Jones. But I didn't get on with science and maths, so I didn't really get on with those teachers. I used to mess around because I didn't understand it.

Were you ever teacher's pet?

Everyone thought I was because I was really into drama. I'd always be the first person to arrive at the drama classes because I really wanted to do it. I got a bit of stick because of that. People would make comments to me; just idiots. But I never actually got bullied in school, and me and my mates would pick on the bullies if they were bullying someone.

It also says in your reports you were popular with your classmates. Is that true?

There was a group of us, and we were like the rulers. Looking back at it we were right saddos, but at the time we thought we were the business. We were popular with all the girls, and you'd get the odd bloke who didn't like that so they'd start on us. But they never got anywhere, we just used to laugh at them.

Did you mess around?

One of your reports says you sometimes acted a little 'silly'... Oh yeah, in science with my mate David Penfold was the worst. We used to get into trouble because we used to egg each other on. We used to flick chewing gum into girls' hair, which was really out of order. I always used to copy everyone's homework in maths as well. No wonder I never did very well in it. I was cheeky, that was my problem.

What was the worst trouble you got into?

We had a teacher who was really, really tall and me and my mates were laughing at him one day and I said he was lanky. He heard me and he went mad and pushed me against the wall and made me stay behind after school. He gave me lines to do and everything. He really scared me, so I didn't do anything that bad after that.

What were your favourite subjects?

Drama, music and English. But I hated science.

Apparently one of your favourite books at junior school was 'A Book Of Cats'. Do you remember it?

Yes, but that was a long time ago! I remember that a lady would be talking on a tape, and you'd have to read the book at the same time so you could learn how to read. I used to read the Billy Blue Hat and Roger Red Hat books as well, and the Happy Family books. I loved all that.

One report says you were good at map reading. Is that still true?

No way! Give me a map now and I'm terrible.

It also says your guitar playing was good. Do you still play now?

No, I gave up man a long time ago because I found it boring. I regret it now because I'm in the music business. I know some chords but I don't know how to strum or anything. I'd like to learn again.

Are you still a good swimmer like your reports say you used to be?

I'm alright. I used to be really good at swimming under water, but for some reason I'm not now.

If you had to write a school report for yourself back in your school days, what would you have said?

I would have said: 'Antony is a very good pupil but he gets easily distracted by certain people, including Andy Murray (who is my best mate) and David Penfold' (my other mate I went to school with). Andy and I are like best mates now, and we go on holiday together and stuff. He's a top bloke.

Not surprisingly Duncan loved performing, and his music lessons, and always got distracted by the girls. Here's his take on what his teachers said...

Dumpton School

Name: D. James
Term: Summer Term 1988
Term Grade: B
Form: 3
No. in Form: 14
Age: 9.9.3.m.
Av. Age: 9.4.3.m.

Subject	Term/Exam	Report
ENGLISH	Term B / Exam 87% / 3rd	Duncan is always so enthusiastic, he has achieved a great deal and done some very pleasing work this term. CR.
FRENCH	Term B / Exam 67% / 5th	Duncan works with terrific enthusiasm and has achieved a good standard. His effort is well rewarded. BB
MATHEMATICS	Term B / Exam 78% / 8th	Duncan is so eager to do well and succeed and has achieved a fairly good standard in the basics. Once set on the right road he is an enthusiastic and quick worker. H
READING	Term / Exam	Duncan enjoys reading and is a pleasure to listen to when reading aloud. CR.
PHYSICS & CHEMISTRY	Term B / Exam 56% / 11th	He has had a good term and I will miss his cheerful rather provocative company. He has great interest in this subject and displays some real ability. I wish him well. CET.
HISTORY	Term B / Exam 54% / 13th	Duncan has participated well in the lessons and has enjoyed studying local history. He has worked well throughout the term, but his exam result was disappointing, in view of his term's work. ASB
GEOGRAPHY	Term A / Exam 60% / 12th	A good term's work, followed by a pleasing exam result. Duncan puts himself completely into his work. Well done. BB
SCRIPTURE	Term C / Exam 75% / 10	His oral work is stronger than his written work and his enthusiasm is still tremendous! JCT.

ART: Duncan enjoys his art lessons and produces some good results. ITG

All Music: Duncan participates actively and quietly. An excellent term. HK.

MUSIC

GAMES: Still an excellent runner and athlete and quite a good cricketer. He gives no trouble at all on the disciplinary side and is a popular member of every team. He will do well as a sportsman. CET.

Form Master/Mistress's Report Days Absent: 1.
Duncan has continued to progress steadily, and has achieved a great deal. I shall miss his cheerful smile and his lively, little voice. I know that he will do well at a Middle School and wish him every happiness and success. CR.

Headmaster's Report
Duncan puts a great deal into all he does and I am sure he will do well. We shall miss him but hope to hear lots of news. ASW

NEXT TERM: Boarders return on 15th September by 15:30
The train leaves Waterloo at 13:22
Day Boys and Pre-Prep return on 16th September
The term ends on 16th December.

What was your favourite subject at school?
I always, always, always loved drama. I loved music as well, and I liked French and English.

What subject did you hate?
I absolutely hated maths, I just didn't get it. I haven't got a brain for calculations and figures. I was never bright academically, but I always excelled in practical things like drama, music and sports. I think that's because I really enjoyed those subjects and I felt comfortable with them.

What did you get told off for most?
Lack of concentration. I had a really short attention span at school, and I still have now. My brain tends to wander off and start thinking about other things. I was always a bit of a daydreamer as well and would end up staring out the window and thinking about stuff when I should have been working. I'd be thinking about what I was going to do that night or planning things rather than getting my work done.

Did you let the girls distract you?

Yes, I always used to get into trouble because of the girls. There was this one girl who I had a big crush on at school. She used to sit behind me in maths, and because I hated maths all I used to do was write notes in my maths book and pass it back to her, then she would write them back to me. I did that in my maths classes for three years.

One of your reports says that you were very self-conscious in your music lessons. Do you think that's because you were so determined to get things right?

Yes, because I really wanted to work hard on my music. My first school was a private school, which I went to from four until nine. My granddad was the head of music and French so I got reduced rates to go there. It was a really good school and my grandparents thought that sending me there would give me a good grounding in life. So I was always very conscious about my music because I wanted to impress Grandpa. I had piano lessons from the age of four until I rebelled and gave up when I was 13. I can still play the piano but unfortunately I can't read music. But I'm really lucky because I can still play stuff by ear, which I've always been able to do.

You seemed to do well in French. Can you still speak it now?

Yes. I've always been good at languages. I really enjoyed them at school.

What do you wish you could change about your school days?

I wish that I'd worked a bit harder for my GCSEs. Looking back I wish I'd made a bit more effort. It hasn't really affected my work because this is what I've always wanted to do, but I still wonder if I could have come out with better grades if I'd paid attention. I wish I'd tried harder – more for me than anything – because I would like to know what I'm capable of. I was always more interested in messing around with my mates than working. I saw school as a social event rather than a learning event. I had great fun at school, but I'd like to go back and put more work in.

Who was your favourite teacher and why?

I had a drama teacher called Angela Davis at Sidmouth College. We had such a good relationship, but then I messed up because I turned up to one of her lessons drunk just before my A-Level exam and she went mad at me. It was really horrible and we drifted apart, but we're back in contact now and I've got a lot of time for her. She gave me the grounding to know what I wanted to do in life.

Were you popular with your classmates?

Yes, I was lucky that I was always very popular at school. When I first went to Sidmouth College – where I went from 13 until 18 – I was the new boy and I was popular with the girls, and some of the blokes hated that. But when I got into the sixth form I had the best school time I'd ever had. My mates were fantastic and I love them to bits. We had such a giggle, and school became so different. I used to love coming into school each day. I had more responsibility and could come and go as I pleased, and I had my motorbike as well so I had total freedom. I loved that.

If you had to write a school report for yourself back in your school days, what would you have said?

Performing was my main focus when I was at school, and because of that all my school reports said the same thing: "Duncan loves socialising and has great enthusiasm, but he's not as good academically as he is practically."

When it comes to his reports, you won't be shocked to read that Lee loved to mess around, was brilliant at writing poetry, and used to gatecrash other people's singing lessons.

THE ITALIA CONTI ACADEMY OF THEATRE ARTS LIMITED

Name: _LEE RYAN_   Subject: _ACTING_

Term/Year: 19_96_

SUMMER

Lee has difficulty in concentrating in performance as well as in rehearsal. As a result, his characterisations suffer and his work becomes sub-standard. He is earnest and I believe he has something to offer but all too often he lets himself down by his behaviour.

He needs to sit down and focus on his desire to become a professional and what this requires — hard work, devotion and determination — without these qualities natural ability becomes flawed and redundant.

Think long and hard!

Teacher: _DAVID BRADSHAWE_

The Italia Conti Academy
of Theatre Arts Ltd

Lee Ryan

Report

1995-96

DIANA'S SONG

Like a crumbled bit of paper thrown upon the floor, Ripped up and savaged, your pain was always more.
The times when you were happy, the times when you were sad, please tell me why the sweet things
turn out so bad.
Your pain was also harder than we could believe,
We picked you up and chucked you away and sold all your grieve.

But tell me why you didn't walk away,
Tell me why you stayed, was it the fact that you

were in love and couldn't walk away?
You told the world your stories and how you were deceived, you lost all your self esteem until you were believed.

Your broken shattered body lay upon our hearts, but it's too late now to say
I'm sorry.
We never took an interest in what you used to do you were blanked out by society and all your family too.
Why didn't we take an interest in what you used to do, if only we could turn back time we would know now what to do.

But tell me why you didn't walk away, tell me why you stayed, was it the fact that you were in love and couldn't walk away?
You told the world your stories and how you were deceived, You lost all your self esteem until you were believed, But tell me why you didn't walk away, tell me why you stayed, was it the that you were in love and couldn't walk away!

Lee Ryan

It's a pity Lee that the setting-out is still not quite right, with the separate lines needing to be set out one line after the other, not running into each other. The content is highly thoughtful, however, and shows what you can produce when you get down to it. You can do better than 7 weeks, Lee — prove it to me, next time!

(2) C:18
(7) P:4
(0) B:8
28
40 C   MERIT AWARD, for quality of content!

Your school reports weren't exactly glowing. Why do you think you messed around so much?
I got frustrated because I couldn't understand the work most of the time. Teachers also used to put me down. I used to argue with one teacher because I was trying to fight my corner, but then the other teachers would come in and start having a go at me as well. It was a nightmare.

What used to distract you at school?
Singing lessons. I used to bunk off my lessons and go to other people's singing lessons. I used to hide at the back so the teacher didn't see me.

According to your reports you used to daydream a lot…
Yeah, the lessons didn't interest me so I'd go off daydreaming. I think school doesn't teach you enough about the future, they only teach you about the past, and that's not helpful. I didn't want to learn about the past, so I used to go off into my own world.

Did you get other people into trouble? Or did they get you into trouble?
Both, really. But I remember when I kicked this can out of the window and it hit the cleaner and this girl got caught laughing at him out of the window. She got blamed, but she never grassed me up. I had respect for that because everyone else used to grass me up and get me into trouble.

What was the worst trouble you got into?
I never did anything really bad. Some kids round my way punched teachers and stuff, but I never did that. I used to get annoyed if kids were being bullied by older kids, so I'd step in and end up in trouble myself.

You studied ballet. What was that like?
To be honest, looking back I quite enjoyed it, but at the time I didn't. When I was at Italia Conti I was more into my singing than my dancing, but I didn't mind doing the dancing as well.

Do you regret messing around when you look back on things?
No, I hated school and I don't regret anything. My diary at school was always filled with red marks where I'd missed a day or got told off. But the thing is, no-one knew I was dyslexic so I didn't really get the help I needed. When I was young I used to cry about it and stuff, but no-one knew what I was going through. In a way school taught me to be myself and not what the teachers wanted me to be. Well, I taught myself really because I saw how fake they were and I made sure that I wasn't anything like them, that's why I'm always myself with people.

We've got one of your poems, Diana . When did you start writing poetry?
I didn't start writing them until I was in my teens. My mum always used to write loads of poems, and she suggested that I tried it one time. I didn't like English so I wasn't really that keen, but then I tried it and I loved it. I used to sing all the time, so then I starting writing songs rather than poems.

Have you kept all your poems?
Yeah, I've got books full of them. Some of them are quite controversial though, and if I ever published them I'd be in so much trouble. They're all about Jesus and God and the government and The Pope. I'd never be able to publish them.

What is 'Diana' about?
Diana was actually a song, I wrote it when Princess Diana died. I liked what Diana stood for.

What do you think poetry has done for you?
It's helped me to write songs. I learnt a lot through writing poetry that I didn't realise I would.

When we looked back on Simon's school reports, we discovered that he was hugely popular with his teachers, loved sports and still goes back to visit his old school now.

City of Birmingham

ST. ANDREWS J.I. SCHOOL.

REPORT ON

Simon Webbe

Tests
Maths – 70/100
Spelling – 15/20
Handwriting – 19/20

Reading – Simon has made some progress with his reading but has been hindered by absence.

English – He has a very active imagination which he puts to full use when writing stories. The ideas he puts forward in discussion are often the starting point for the rest of the class.

Maths – Simon is slow to complete his written maths but always gets there in the end. He enjoys practical activities and can be relied upon to work on his own without supervision.

General – He has made steady progress in all areas. Simon excels at all sports especially gymnastics and football.

DATE 5th JULY 1987   CLASS TEACHER S.F. Hughes
ATTENDANCE 19 days' absence
PUNCTUALITY Good   HEAD TEACHER M.A. Fawcett

THE NEW SCHOOL YEAR BEGINS ON 3rd SEPTEMBER 1987

City of Birmingham

ST. ANDREWS J.I. SCHOOL.

REPORT ON

Simon Webbe.

Mathematics 92/100
Spelling 19/20
Handwriting 16/20

Reading :– I am delighted with Simon's progress. Initially he was rather hesitant but now reads quite fluently and with expression. He takes great pleasure in mastering 'new long' words and enjoys reading poetry.

English :– Very pleasing progress. Simon works independently without fuss, completing his language tasks quickly and accurately. However he is still a little reluctant to develop his own ideas in creative writing. His work is always neatly presented and he participates eagerly in all oral work offering pertinent and original ideas.

Mathematics :– I am delighted with the rapid progress Simon has made this year. He has worked very hard and deserves his excellent results in the mathematic examination. Well done Simon.

General :– A very pleasing year's work. Simon has responded most positively to being taught in a small group. He is always very pleasant and polite and very quick to help others. He relates well to adults and enjoys sound friendships with other children. He is a most valued member of the school football team. I have enjoyed teaching him. Well done Simon.

DATE 10th JULY   CLASS TEACHER H.M. Metcalfe
ATTENDANCE 2 days' absence
PUNCTUALITY Very Good.   HEAD TEACHER M.A. Fawcett

THE NEW SCHOOL YEAR BEGINS ON 2nd SEPTEMBER

Birmingham Schools' Football Association

LEAGUE WINNERS

This is to Certify that
Simon Webbe
was a team member of
St. Andrew's school,
the League Champions of the
Belchers Lane Division
of the B.S.F.A. in the Season 1987-88.
Signed M.A. Fawcett   Team Manager
Date: April 1988.

What was your favourite subject at school?
Drama, and obviously PE because I love football. I loved all physical sports. I'm not a fan of cricket, but I'd play it because we were made to by the PE teacher.

What subjects did you hate?
I didn't really hate anything. I wasn't particularly good at French and maths, but I never dreaded going to the lessons or anything. I loved school. Education is really important and I didn't do as much as I should have or would have liked to have done because I allowed myself to be led

simon

astray. When I was a young I was always one of those kids who wanted to do the right thing, but didn't always do it. I was always looking for a way to get out of doing the work!

What did you get told off for most?
I would get told off for being smart, and for rolling my eyes at teachers. And if a teacher shouted at me I would say, "Would you shout at me if my mum was here? I don't think so." If someone raises their voice to me I switch off. I hate people raising their voices because sometimes it makes me raise my voice back. I only got into trouble for messing around, really. I remember when I was shaking my mate's hand once I yanked it for a joke, and I pulled his arm out of its socket. Obviously I didn't mean to do it but I didn't know my own strength. It was one of those things that everyone used to do for a laugh, but it went too far. I never meant to do bad things, I just used to mess around too much.

From reading your reports it seems like all your teachers really liked you…
Yeah, they did. Especially the headmaster. I was headboy, and in a way I didn't want to do it, but I was voted in. I was captain of the football team and stuff, but I didn't want people to be jealous of me because I was headboy, and unfortunately that did happen. Also, it gave me more responsibility that I didn't want. I wanted to play football at dinner times and stuff, and I had to sacrifice that sometimes because I had headboy stuff to do.

Did you let the girls distract you in school?
Put it this way, when it came down to choosing which subjects you wanted to do, I chose what the girls chose!

One of your reports says you had 'sound friendships'. Were you popular with your classmates?
I wasn't a leader or anything like that, but I was quite popular. I was into getting along with people, but there were always those people who wanted to stir up trouble. It was weird

because the bullies were the people other people always clung to because they didn't want to be their enemy. They always say you keep your friends close but your enemies closer, and that's so true. I had a really good group of mates I always went round with at breaktimes: Darren Archer, Warren Gordon, Antony Downs, Julian Patrick, Brendan Herron, Gavin Exhall, Martin Lally, Meetesh Palmer and Rory McGowen. I still keep in touch with Rory, Meetesh, Brendan, Julian and Antony.

Who was your favourite teacher and why?
I had a lot of brilliant teachers, I liked all the teachers at my school. I had a good relationship with all of them. I got on well with my history, drama and PE teachers, who were all female. I got along with all the female teachers particularly well, but I did get on with the guys too. I really fancied my history teacher big time. She was lovely!

What do you think your teachers think of your success?
They're proud of me. I still go back to see them. I went back a while ago and took my little girl in and introduced her to my teachers. Hopefully she'll go to that school. They've still got pictures of me in the school, and I've still got a good relationship with the teachers. It still smells the same when I go back there, and it brings back memories of playing football on the tarmac.

What do you wish you could change about your school days?
We all put this one kid through hell for two months and I really regret that. It wasn't a very nice thing to do.

If you had to write a school report for yourself back in your school days, what would you have said?
I was pretty well behaved in school, and I would have said: "Simon has the ability to learn and is very easily distracted, but is a good boy."

love

First kisses, making girl's sick, losing their virginity,
and marriage plans. Blue reveal everything about love.

My first ever girlfriend was a girl at school called Louise. She used to go to Roe Green in Kingsbury, North West London, and me and my best friend Andrew fancied her. We used to play kiss chase with her in the playground. We'd say that whoever caught her and kissed her first was her boyfriend. I got the first kiss off her so that meant that I was her boyfriend. We used to do this fake marriage thing in the playground as well. I once married her at the beginning of lunchtime but we'd split by the end of it. My first official girlfriend was called Kelly and she'll kill me when she reads this! I went to Hendon school with her and she was my girlfriend from the summer of 1993 to October 1993. I had my first proper snog with her when we were playing spin the bottle. It was quite weird because I'd seen the film Grease and I thought that the way Danny Zuko kissed a girl was how you did it – you know, when he takes off his ring and gives it to her and put his arm around her? I learnt pretty quickly it

wasn't, though. Kissing has changed a lot since those days. Some girls have said that I'm quite a good kisser, which is always nice. I need to get some more practice in though, so any offers are gratefully received! I'd give myself a six out of ten as a kisser I reckon. I'm not going to go around saying that I'm the best kisser in the world and that girls have to kiss me because I'm so good, but it is nice if they say I am. I was 18 when I lost my virginity. It was a week after my 18th birthday. All my mates had lost theirs when they were about 16 or 17, and I thought I was weird because I hadn't lost it. But in the end I thought, "Do you know what? I'll lose it when I lose it." I think 18 was a good age for me to lose my virginity. I don't agree with people having sex under 16, I don't think that's right at all. And I think it's so bad that kids are concerned about sex at ten or eleven. They should be concentrating on school and be allowed to be kids. Girlfriends and boyfriends will always be around so there's no rush. I think it's nicer to wait.

When people ask me if I've ever been in love I'm not sure what to say. What is love? I've thought I've been in love in the past but then I've finished with girls and after that I haven't stayed friends with them, so I can't have been. It's a hard question. I think I'll know when I fall in love. I think that everyone has a different way of showing their feelings where love is concerned. When I thought I was in love it really changed me as a person. I'm usually quite a strong person, and it made me go all soft and I did everything the girl said, which wasn't like me at all. This one girl used to have mood swings on me all the time, and I would still be like, "Are you alright, are you alright?" and really worrying about it. Then the next minute she would be fine and I would be really confused. I kind of thought to myself, "What am I doing?" You put up with a lot when you like someone though. And then when someone's really nice to you, you don't like them. It's mad. I don't know if I'm ready to settle down with a girlfriend yet. I'm still having fun. It's a mad situation to be in if you've got a girlfriend, and things are going mental at the moment so I don't think it would be fair on the girl or me.

Even though I've never been in love I would say I have had my heart broken. Well not so much broken, I was just really gutted about this girl. I was with her for about five months when I was 16 and I always thought she fancied my mate because they were flirting and everything while I was still with her. Then as soon as we split up they got together. I never found out if anything was actually going on when we were together and I don't think I want to know. I'm not normally a jealous person but I felt really weird when that happened. But I just left it. If I see them around now I say hello to them both, but they're not my drinking partners or anything. Even though that was pretty upsetting, I am lucky in that I've never been dumped. It's not an ego thing, I just always seem to get in there first. The worst way I've dumped a girl was at school when my mate David dared me to dump my girlfriend over the balcony at lunchtime. I was about 11 at the time and I shouted her name and said, "You're dumped!" I thought I was well hard but she started crying her eyes out. I said sorry to her and all that, but she was so upset. It's funny to look back on it because we're still mates and she still reminds me of it all the time. She always says to me, "You may be famous, but I still remember when you dumped me." She always brings it up. I remember this other time when I was seeing these two girls at the same time and I didn't realise they were mates. So I took this one girl to a club and then this other girl walked in, and it all kicked off. I just walked away. I was like, "Hands up, I've been caught red-handed. Simple as that." I wouldn't two time a girl now though, it would be too much hassle. If I did it now it would be in the papers and all that, and it ain't worth the hassle. I would never be able to get away with it! And I wouldn't want to do it now anyway.

When I'm going out with a girl I am romantic in my own way. I'm not a chocolate and flowers man though, I'm more a 'take a girl out and have a good time' man. Some guys will write poems and love songs and give girls chocolates and take them to the best restaurants, but that's not me. I'm not into all that. I like to take a girl out to a club and have a laugh. And as long as a girl's having a good time it pleases me. It's more relaxed than going to a suave restaurant and spending £250 on dinner. I mean, for what? I do like to give presents though. I once bought a girl a necklace with a sapphire stone in it. It was nice and she looked lovely in it. Very sexy. The best present I ever got was a Gucci ring a girlfriend gave me one Christmas, which was wicked.

When it comes to women, I like a girl who likes to have a good time. And a girl's eyes and mouth and teeth are important. And I like nice legs and feet. I'm a foot and shoe man. I always thought I was weird, but when the band got together I was talking to Simon about what kind of girls we like, and when he said he liked feet. I was like, "Oh my god, I'm not the only weird one!" Our tour manager Johnny likes girls' feet as well. We all look at them in the street and Duncan and Lee think we're weird. We're always like, "You don't understand. If a girl's got nasty feet, forget it!" I also like a girl who walks into a room and brightens it up. I like a girl that you could take to a party and not have to babysit her. I like it if a girl can look after herself and hold her own in a room. That's more of a turn-on than a girl being pretty but not talking to my mates; I'm not into any of that. I think basically I want someone who's the same as me. Someone who's strong headed but likes to have a laugh.

I do fancy some female celebs, but I haven't got any more chance of getting together with them than anyone else. I think Rachel from S Club is pretty, and Tyler from allSTARS is very pretty, she looks very Mediterranean. And I think Britney Spears is gorgeous obviously, and Sandra Bullock because she's not stunning. Sandra Bullock is a natural beauty and you could take her home to meet your mum. I like natural girls like her. Stunning girls scare me. You don't want to be yourself because you don't know how they'll react. I've been linked with Jessica from Liberty X before but we're just mates. We share the same birthday, which is cool – 23rd June by the way! All that happened is that I was talking to her in a bar on the Smash Hits roadshow, and the next thing you know I was linked with her in the press. I was gobsmacked. But the papers have got to fill their pages!

I know straight off when girls like me because they like the band. I know when they're not after the real me; when they're just after a pop star. And sometimes when people find out what you're really like they're like, "Why aren't you like you are on TV?" It's like, "Er, because I'm human!" I just have a laugh with it and I don't take it too seriously. I'm starting to get texts on my phone from people saying that their friend fancies me or whatever, and I don't even know them. People

get hold of my number somehow, and I know those girls only like me because of the band. I was wary of girls even before I was in the band, I was always careful anyway, and now I'm even more careful. I like a girl who doesn't talk about my work and isn't fazed by it. I don't know if I would date a fan, but I would never say never, I could certainly date someone that likes our music. Why not? We've got some gorgeous fans.

I know without a doubt that I want to get married and have kids one day. I'd like to do it before I'm 30, really, but it depends on what I'm doing. I hope I'm still with the band, and if not I'd like to be doing other things in the entertainment world. I'm not sure how many kids I want, but I would say three. My mum's had three - me, my brother and my sister - so I'd like the same. It worked pretty well for us!

The first girl I would call my proper girlfriend was a girl I met when I was at middle school. I was about nine or ten and I went out with her for about a year and half. She was called Sorrel and my best friend went out with her best mate Kelly, so we always all went around together. Then after about a year and a half we swapped and I went out with Kelly and he went out with Sorrel. I learnt how to kiss with Sorrel, she was the first girl that I properly snogged. I remember

my best mate saying to me that kissing was like chewing grass. He told me to get a bit of grass and chew it and that would help me to be a good kisser. Believe it or not I did actually chew grass to find out what he meant, but I'm not sure it helped my technique. He also used to tell me to practise on my hand and in the mirror, so I used to go home and practise and then try it out on Sorrel the next day. But I am a good kisser now, honest! I think kissing becomes different as you get older, it changes a lot. It's a sensuous thing now. I don't think, "I'm going to kiss you now," about someone. I don't plan it; it's a natural thing. I'm always told I'm quite a sensuous kisser. I've got soft lips and I've never had any complaints!

People often ask me if I've ever been in love, and I have. Well, I think you can call it love. Then again, I'm not sure I know what love is because I haven't really experience proper, all-out, full-on love. It's weird, I suppose you don't know until you're in it. I thought I'd been in love with a couple of girls in the past. One who was really special was a Spanish girl called Matilda who I met when I was 15. She came over to England every summer for three years, and the whole year I would wait for her to arrive and get really excited. I genuinely thought I was in love with her. I loved the way I felt but I can't describe it. It's just that amazing feeling when you're with someone your heart is racing. And when you meet them and speak to them on the phone you get this feeling. You just know that you really like them and you can't wait for them to call. I love that feeling but it doesn't happen often. It doesn't seem to happen as much as you get older which is a real shame. I've never been in love in a sexual relationship, though. I've come close to it and I've thought, "I really really like you," but something's gone horribly wrong and it hasn't worked out. I lost my virginity a week before my 18th birthday and it was a drunken mess. I was actually one of the last of my mates to lose my

duncan

virginity. I was always paranoid that something bad would happen to me when I did lose it because I'm a Catholic boy. I still worry now, it's the guilt thing. I experimented and did other stuff growing up but I'd never been all the way, then one day it happened and I lost my virginity. I remember thinking the next day, "My god, I'm not a virgin anymore!" I was walking around in a daydream. It was so weird. I know a lot of my mates lost it at about 16 but I think that's too young. Eighteen was a good age for me and I definitely think I was right to wait.

Love is brilliant, but it can also be really painful and I have had my heart broken in the past. There was this girl that I thought I was in love with called Tina. I really liked her and fell for her in a big way, but I was really cautious with her because I really liked her but I was scared of falling in love and making a commitment. We were picking up vibes from each other, but I introduced her to my mate Phil and he ended up getting it on with her. I actually caught them together and I was devastated. I never blamed Phil, I was angry with her and for some reason I took it all out on her. I met up with her recently and I told her how gutted I was at the time and she said she was sorry and everything. So it's cool now, we're just mates and there are no feelings there anymore. There was another girl that I had a crush on for about five years, and I still know her now. She was three years older than I was and from the age of about ten to 15, every time she walked past the house I would go running after her. I thought she was great. I used to write her letters all the time saying how much I loved her. Every Sunday after church my grandfather would take me to the shop to buy some sweets, and I would always get him to buy me a chocolate heart or something. Then I would get a teddy bear and put the chocolate heart in its lap and run after her and give it to her. I never did get to go out with her even after all that, which was a bit gutting!

As well as having my heart broken I think I've probably broken a few along the way as I haven't always dumped people in the nicest way. I remember at school we used to call it 'chucking someone' and it was all over very quickly. You could chuck someone halfway through a lesson and it wouldn't matter. I remember splitting up with a girl and I had to tell her over the phone because face to face would have been too hard. I remember telling her that I really liked her but I didn't think it was working and she got

pretty upset. I also got caught red-handed two-timing a girl when I was younger. I was seeing a girl in Sidmouth and I was in a local nightclub when she caught me snogging another girl. That was pretty bad. There have also been other times when I've had two girls on the go at the same time, but that's the only time I've been caught.

I think I am romantic when I'm going out with a girl. In fact, I think I'm very romantic. I like going out for dinner with a woman and wining and dining and spoiling her. I like a nice candlelit meal,

and I love to take women out and spend money on them and treat them like a princess. I'm a bit old fashioned like that. I'm a gentleman, really. I think the most romantic thing I've ever done was when I took out a girl for a really nice meal at San Lorenzo's in London, which is a really posh restaurant. I bought her champagne and some flowers and a present and she was really touched. There are so many romantic things I think about doing, but because I haven't really had a girlfriend to be romantic with for a long time. It's a shame because I would love to do the whole romantic weekend break thing with someone. I was actually seeing someone before I got into the band, but she couldn't handle the fact that there were girls around me and everything, so she finished it. It's a real shame it didn't work out, but I guess it

was for the best in some ways. When I am in a relationship I love being given presents, like teddy bears and letters. I love letters, and I've kept all mine from when I was younger, as well as all my valentine cards and stuff. I think I am pretty soft hearted really.

When it comes to girls, I only fall for girls I get a good vibe about. I'm a good judge of character and I'm good at reading people. I wouldn't say I want a particular look in a girl. She's got to have nice eyes because I think eyes tell you a lot about a person's soul, and you can tell a lot about what they're like as a person. They say the eyes are the key to a person's soul and I definitely agree with that. You can look at someone and tell a lot about them. I look at people's inner soul and I can tell a lot about them. I can sometimes predict someone's star sign when I don't even know them because I know their type. I'm very intuitive and I pick up a lot of stuff. I like sweet innocent girls that have something underneath. You know, when you can tell by seeing the twinkle in their eyes that there's more to them. I also like a nice smile, and I think teeth are important. I like a nice personality, and my pet hate is thick girls. It doesn't matter how pretty a girl is – if she's thick, forget it. You've got to be able to hold a conversation with someone. I've got a lot of depth and I think a girl's got to be equally tuned into the stuff I'm into. I'm quite spiritual, and I'm a thinker. I think all the time. I couldn't handle going out with someone who had nothing to say.

Britney Spears is my ideal woman. I met her at the premier of Crossroads and she's got a nice smile, nice teeth, and nice eyes, and she's got that thing going on when she's got a little twinkle in her eye and you know she's really not that innocent! You know when you put someone on a pedestal and you think they may not live up to your expectations? I did that with Geri Haliwell, she just didn't do it for me when I met her. But Britney was everything I expected her to be. She was standing at this party with a drink in her hand and she was grooving to the music and you could tell she just wanted to party. I feel quite sorry for her because she's kept in a shell, but you know she's a party girl underneath it all and she just wants to let herself go. I also think Rachel from S Club is very pretty and has that naughty side to her, but sadly she's taken. I've been linked with a lot of celebrity girls, like Dani Behr, Marie from A*Teens, and Michelle from Liberty X, and I have to admit I've snogged all three! So there was an element of truth in the rumours about me dating them, but it's not like they were my girlfriends. Me and Dani Behr are great mates, though. We were both just drunk one night and ended up snogging, which was quite amusing. We both just laughed about it afterwards, but it got into the papers, so... You can't breathe without things getting into the papers!

With Marie from A*Teens it's a bit different from other girls because I've got a lot of time for her. I think she's a really lovely girl. In her I've met someone that I can really talk to and get on really closely with. But she's really busy doing her own thing, and I'm really busy doing mine, and she lives in Sweden and America, so it's really difficult to get anything serious going between us. We've accepted the fact that we both have a lot of feelings for each other and we're really close, but there's nothing we can do about it at the moment. Who knows what will happen in the future? If we're both single then we may just give it a go. I've seen her a few times and we've had a little snog and stuff which is nice, but we're just friends at the moment. We really understand each other and what each other is going through which is fantastic. I really hope to settle down and have kids one day. I want to have three kids at least. I'd like to get married around 28-30, or at least be settled down by then. I don't want to be an old dad. I want to be a young dad so I can really enjoy spending time with my kids. I can't wait for all that; it's so exciting.

Looking back I had quite a few girlfriends when I was younger. My first girlfriend was called Hayley, and I went out with her when I was about eight. She was really nice, but I used to fancy loads of other girls as well, so we didn't last that long. I can't remember my actual first kiss that well, but I know it was with Hayley. I remember that she was sick because I stuck my tongue down her throat. I thought that's how you were supposed to kiss. I think when you're young you don't really know what you're doing. Kissing has really changed a lot since those days - at least I don't make girls sick anymore! I was pretty young when I lost my virginity. I think I just really wanted to get it out of the way. You know, I wanted to get it over and done with. At the time I thought it was the right time for me, but it was really young.

I'm not really looking for love at the moment, I'm kind of having fun. But if I found someone I liked, then great. I'm not sure if I've been in love before, but I've definitely been in lust. I don't know how you know if you're in love, so I guess that means it hasn't happened to me yet.

lee

There have been times when I've thought I was in love, but then when I've split up with people I've realised that I can't have been. I can't understand how love can sum up everything that you feel for someone anyway. I find that really strange that you can lump all those feelings into one word. It doesn't make sense to me. My last couple of girlfriends have been my most serious ones. I went out with a girl a while ago called Carlie that I really liked. I thought we were going to go somewhere but she finished with me and I was gutted. I'm not sure if I've had my heart properly broken, though. I've been upset about girls before, but it's never taken me that long to get over someone. I've never really found myself sitting in feeling sorry for myself or anything. Then again, there was this one girl I really liked and I used to really kick myself about her. I'd be walking down the street and suddenly remember something about her and feel gutted. That went on for quite a while and it felt horrible, so I was obviously pretty hurt when we split up.

When it comes to dumping girls, I'm not very good at all. I always say to them that I'm not good enough for them and try to convince them that they don't want to be with me. Basically, I try to get them to finish with me. I've never been dumped really horribly, I've always been pretty lucky. Of course I've had girls say they don't want to go out with me anymore, but I suppose that's normal and it happens to everyone. The worst time I was dumped was the day I got expelled from school. When I got home my girlfriend at the time, Jemma, rang me up and said she didn't want to go out with me anymore. I was not having a good day. She said she was really sorry for finishing with me but it didn't help. It's a shame because she was a nice girl and she was fit. She went back out with my mate Tony after that which was a bit gutting. I think I'm a good boyfriend but I have two-timed girls in the past. What's a man meant to do when there are so many women around? Girls always blame the men, but I've been out with girls who are seeing other guys as well, so you can't always blame us. And there have been times when I've turned girls down because they've got a bloke, so I'm not all bad!

When I'm with a girl I try to be romantic, but I'm not naturally romantic. I like to buy girls presents and take them out for dinner and stuff. I think going for dinner is a really good way to spend a date. I would never take a girl to a club if we were on a date. What's the point in that? You can't talk to each other and you spend the whole night shouting at each other, which isn't much good when you're trying to get to know one another. Thinking about it, I have done a lot of romantic things in the past. I think the most romantic thing was when I was in a cab with this girl and I got the cab to pull over – and you know those blokes that sell roses on the side of the road? – I bought the lot off him. I gave him about a hundred quid or something and took every single one. But it was worth it. She was really pleased.

I don't think I have a particular type of girl that I go for. I do like blonde girls a lot, but then again I'm into dark-haired girls as well. I'm not that fussy. I just like girls. But I do like a girl to have a personality. That's really important. But sometimes it can be more of a challenge if they don't have a personality. It's quite a challenge if a girl's quiet because you can make them interesting. I like shy girls. But then again I like loud girls. I don't know! I just like women full stop. I can tell straight away if a girl is just after me because of the band. I would date a fan though, but not if they had my name tattooed on their arm or something! That would be a bit weird. But if they're a fan of the music, then that's good. We've got a lot of good-looking fans, so why not? We get to meet a lot of celebrities, but I don't really fancy many celebrity girls, and I would never fancy a girl just because they're famous. People say that pop stars go out with other pop stars because they understand what you're going through, but they don't always. I've been linked with a few celebrity girls, like Liz from Atomic Kitten and the Hear'Say girls, but the only one that's true is Liz. We did see each other for a bit and we still see each other occasionally, but it's so hard to keep a relationship going.

I really like the idea of settling down one day, but I'm not ready just yet. I like steady relationships and I love the feeling of being in a relationship, but I've got two different brains – one brain wants

to settle down with a girl, then the other one wants to go off and do my own thing and be on my own and be a party animal. One day I may wake up and think, "I really want to settle down and have kids and get married." Then the next day I'll be like, "You mug, what are you thinking? You don't want to do that!" It's like I'm two people, and there's always this one in the background telling me I'm better off single. But I suppose you never know when someone will come along. I've still got a good 30 years to find someone and settle down, and I don't want to look back and regret not having had a good time because I was going out with someone the whole time. That's the last thing I want. There's plenty of time for marriage and all that, and one day I do want to have kids and settle down. I think it's important. I'd like a dog as well, a Rottweiler. But I can't have kids and a Rottweiler, so I guess I'll have to make a decision!

lee

simon

My first ever girlfriend was a girl called Denise when I was about four or five. I was going out with her and her best friend at the same time - but that's what they wanted, honest. I've been in demand since the age of four! I only went out with them for about a day and then they dumped me. I was quite gutted actually. I think that was my first taste of real disappointment. I knew one of them still liked me and wanted me for herself, so she convinced the other one to dump so she could have me, but I didn't like her, I liked the other one. It was all very confusing, and in the end I didn't go out with either of them again. I have to have the best or have nothing. I will never settle for second best. I would rather have nothing than second best.

My first grown up girlfriend was a girl called Lisa Riley who I went out with when I was 15. I'd had girlfriends before her but she was my first proper relationship. We were together for three months, but then my mate stepped in and went out with her for two years. We didn't fall out over it or anything, but I was gutted at the time. I'm still gutted to this day in some way because I found out that she finished with me for a reason that wasn't true. She thought I was cheating on her, but I wasn't. I like female company, that's just the way I am. Even now I think if I was going out with a girl now she wouldn't like it because I have got a lot of female friends. But it doesn't mean anything. That's just me. Funnily enough Lisa is one of my best mates now and we talk all the time. Me and her can talk about anything, literally. We go over old times and stuff, and we've got that relationship where nothing can split us up. We'll always be mates and she means a lot to me.

I had my first kiss when I was nine with a girl called Charmaine, and it was really nice. Then my first French kiss was with a girl called Lisa that I went out with for about two weeks. I'd like to think I've got better at kissing since those days. I've certainly never had any complaints. Well, not to my face anyway! I couldn't take it if someone said something like that to my face, it would be awful. As for love, I've been in love plenty of times. I fall in love every day. I'm a sucker for a pretty face. My heart melts and... I hate seeing pretty girls because I know I can't have them. I can't have a relationship at the moment, it's just impossible, so it drives me mad seeing pretty girls everywhere I go. We saw this girl at the airport the other day who was beautiful. Everyone was flocking around her but I stayed away because I knew I couldn't have her, so what's the point in talking to her? I'll only be disappointed.

The first time I properly fell in love was at the age of 17. I was with this girl for two years and it just didn't work out, we were total opposites. She was older than me – about 22, 23 – and she kept telling me to go and have fun because she didn't want to tie me down. She thought I was too young. But I was in love with her and I was so upset about that relationship ending. I don't see her anymore but I would like to. I don't bear any grudges, and it would just be nice to still be in touch with her. Looking back if I had stayed in that relationship I wouldn't be the person I am now. I wouldn't have had the success I've had. I would probably be working three or four jobs trying to keep her happy. That wouldn't have been the life I wanted so things did work out for the best.

The worst way I've ever been dumped is to my face, without any explanation. That's the worst thing; when someone says they don't like you any more but don't give you a reason. I hate that. It's not enough to just tell someone you don't like them. I later found out that this one girl that finished with me did it because she was under pressure from her friends because they thought she was spending too much time with me. I would much rather she had been honest about that than just said she didn't like me because that really hurts. I find it really hard finishing with girls, or even turning them down in the first place. If a girl asks me out, even if I don't really like her I say yes because I feel bad because I know what it's like to be hurt. When I was younger I could never finish with girls. I just wouldn't phone them and hope they got the hint, which is pretty bad I know. I just couldn't face upsetting them. I wasn't very good at being faithful when I was younger either, and never minded two-timing, I once eight-timed a girl! When I was about 16 I had a girl for every day of the week and two girls for Sunday. As I said before, I just like company! Sometimes it did get confusing, but if I couldn't remember the girl's name I would call her babes. All through school I didn't have many girlfriends, I was more interested in football and not really bothered about girls. Then when I left school I discovered women, and that was it, there was no turning back. I lost my virginity when I was 16 and I wish I'd left it a bit later and concentrated on football because as soon as I lost my virginity other things went out the window a bit. I regret that.

I'm not naturally romantic when I'm in a relationship, I have to make the effort. It doesn't automatically come into my head to buy flowers and things, I would have to think about it in advance. What you see with me is what you get. I'm not gong to say I'm Romeo, but I do know how to treat a girl. I like to take a girl to a nice seafood restaurant or a Thai restaurant, I would always see where she wanted to go. And if things got serious, I would take her to my mum's. She's got to pass the test! And if a girl can cook like my mum – hell yeah – I'm all hers! When it comes to women, I love girls that are forward and strong and will say to a man, "I'm having you and you've got no choice." But I also like a girl to let a man be a man and know when to be quiet if you're arguing. There's nothing worse than a girl going on and on and pushing you when you're arguing. I like it if a girl knows when to stop. When it comes to looks I'm not a fussy person. Black, white, Asian... I'm not bothered. I'm just a sucker for a pretty face. I love women. That's what I was put on this earth to do – share love! I've got a real thing for Alicia Keys. We had a connection at cd:uk. We double took each other but we didn't have time to talk. She was so beautiful, but we couldn't speak because we were being pushed in the other direction. But I would like a girl just like her. I also think Christina Milian is cute. As I say, I'm a sucker for a sweet face.

I do know when girls want me just because I'm in Blue. You say hello to girls and they do a double take when they realise who you are, and you can see it in their eyes. It's like, "Ching, ching!" But I don't really expose myself to those sort of girls. I always go to bed early even if we're in other countries, so I don't see the girls hanging around. We have regular fans that we know that come and see us, and we have drinks with some of them in the bar or something and they're cool, but I'm always the first to go to bed. I'm not saying I wouldn't date a fan, there are plenty I would date, but it's most important for them to be a fan of the music. That would be scary. But I would love to make their dream come true in the same way I would have liked Janet Jackson to make my dreams come true when I was younger.

I am planning to get married one day. I would like to settle down and have a family, all of it. I want to have businesses and things that I can hand over to my kids to set them up. It's definitely something I'm looking forward to.

just chillin'

Even uber-busy pop stars get the odd day off to hang out with their mates and chill. Here we discover how Blue like to unwind and escape the stresses of being in the biggest pop band in Britain…

simon

How do you relax?

I go to my studio. I've got my own little studio and that helps me to get away from things.
It's my escape.

Do you play golf/go fishing, etc?

No. But when things start calming down, once a month me and the boys are going to meet up
and go bowling or fishing or something.

What was the last...

Book you read?

I don't read. I watch DVDs all day.

Film you watched?

A film called Scorpion. I love old Asian movies that are dubbed over.

CD you listened to?

It was a demo that I did last night.

TV programme you watched?

I love all the soaps, so it was one of them.

What is your all-time favourite ...

Film?

Fist Of Legend with Jet Lee.

Book?

None, really.

TV Show?

Diff'rent Strokes.

Album?

112, Part III.

Who do you like to chill out with?

My crew, my friends and my band.

How do you totally de-stress?

I've got this thing that I do where instead of getting angry, I go into myself and talk to myself.
I tell myself that how I'm feeling at that moment isn't how I'm going to be feeling the next day
or week. So I just deal with things and that de-stresses me.

Are you into therapies, like massage?

Hell yeah! I love massage, it's so relaxing.

How much sleep do you need?

Oh man, I could sleep for England. I could literally get up and have breakfast, go back to sleep, get up and have lunch, go back to sleep… I love sleeping.

What position do you sleep in?

I'm a weird sleeper. I toss and turn until I find my spot. If I'm in a deep sleep I usually sleep on my side. I could balance on the edge of a bed and not move for eight hours if I wanted to.

Where is your favourite place to escape to?

I haven't got anywhere really, but I would love to get myself a place abroad somewhere at some point.

Where is your favourite holiday destination?

The Caribbean. And I really like LA.

Where would you love to go on holiday?

Africa. I would like to tour the whole country, but not get ill!

If you could be anywhere relaxing right now, where would you be and who would you be with?

I'd be on a beach somewhere with my little girl, spending some quality time in the sun. And I'd like my brother and sister to be there too.

antony

How do you relax?

If I can I like to see my mates. I'll go out with my mate George and see what's going on with him. I like to see my family as well.

Do you play golf/go fishing, etc?

No, I'm not into any of that.

What was the last...

Book you read?

Lenny McLean, The Guv'nor. I've got this real thing about old gangster books.
They fascinate me. I love to find out what went on with gangsters in the 60s and early 50s.

Film you watched?

The Ninth Gate with Johnny Depp. It was absolute rubbish. I don't rate him at all. I think he's useless, he's just not a warm character.

CD you listened to?

The Best of Earth, Wind and Fire.

TV programme you watched?

Only Fools and Horses.

What is your all-time favourite...

Film?

Grease. I'm a massive Grease fan.

Book?

Lenny McLean, The Guv'nor.

TV show?

Only Fools and Horses.

Album?

The best of George Michael or The Best of Earth, Wind and Fire.

Who do you like to chill out with?

George, Andy, Chris, Simon and Nick. We've got this minute by minute crew when we go out
and get drunk. We've got this little vibe going.

How do you totally de-stress?

I make sure I don't think about work. I think if you take your work home with you, you don't have
a life. You have to learn when to switch off. That's why I don't often go to the showbiz parties,
because I end up talking about work all the time. I do really enjoy going to some of them,
but I have to be in the right mood.

Are you into therapies, like massage?

I love massage, I don't get enough of it. I want to make a point of getting one every couple of weeks because I've got a bad back. I'd like a nice girl to give me a massage!

How much sleep do you need?

On average six to eight hours. I used to be good at getting up in the mornings, but I'm always so tired these days. I sleep whenever and wherever I can now.

What position do you sleep in?

I sleep on my side with my right hand under the pillow.

Where is your favourite place to escape to?

I live in Hertfordshire so it's like being in the country. There are a few nice country pubs down there and stuff, so I can relax with my mates.

What is your favourite holiday destination?

Cyprus. I went in May and I had a giggle. I'm Greek and I've got a few cousins out there, so if I ever get hassle they're there to sort it out.

Where would you love to go on holiday?

Barbados.

If you could be anywhere relaxing right now, where would you be and who would you be with?

I'd like to be in the sun by a pool somewhere, reading my gangster book. As for who I'd like to be with? That would be telling!

duncan

How do you relax?

I like just going round to my mates' houses and doing nothing. Lying in front of the TV and watching a movie, and just doing normal stuff. That chills me out.

Do you play golf/go fishing, etc?

No, but I like playing tennis. I was playing tennis with Gary Barlow at his mansion the other day and I beat him!

What was the last...

Book you read?

The Harry Potter books.

Film you watched?

The Ninth Gate with Johnny Depp. It's all about evil spirits. I thought it was a good film.

CD you listened to?

At the moment I'm listening to some new Blue stuff. I'm really proud of it.

TV programme you watched?

Big Brother.

What is your all-time favourite...

Film?

The Matrix, and I love The Fifth Element.

Book?

I loved the Harry Potter books. I'm not a huge reader but I got really into them.

TV show?

Star Trek Voyager and Friends.

Album?

I was really impressed with Natalie Imbruglia's Left of The Middle album, and also Mel C's Northern Star. And Sheryl Crowe's album The Globe Sessions is fantastic.

Who do you like to chill out with?

My mates. I've got a handful of really great mates, a circle of close friends. They know who they are and I appreciate them very much. They accept me for still being me even thought my life's totally changed.

How do you totally de-stress?

I like going to church when I get time. When it all gets too much for me and I have time off, I'll go back to Dorset and go to the graveyard and sit by my grandparent's grave for a few hours. I cry my eyes out and I get everything out, and I come away feeling so revived. I feel great because I've talked to them. That's like my spiritual healing.

Are you into therapies, like massage?

Yes, I like the whole massage, herbal essences, spiritual healing thing.

How much sleep do you need?

At the least, seven hours. Ideally I need about eight or nine hours to function, but I can cope with seven. I've even learnt to survive with six, and sometimes we'll only get about three or four.

What position do you sleep in?

Curled up on my right.

Where is your favourite place to escape to?

I love going down to Dorset. I go and stay with my friend Sam who is in her 30s and pretty hippy. She's very new age and her house has such a chilled vibe with crystals and wind chimes and things everywhere. I go down there with my mates and sit and chill.

Where is your favourite holiday destination?

Anywhere as long as I'm with my family and friends. I've been on a couple of cruises which I've really enjoyed because you get to see a lot of different places. I'm also really drawn to Italy and Spain. I think my father is three quarters Italian, and my mum has some Italian blood in her, so I have a lot of Italian blood in me. When I go to Italy I get the feeling that I belong.

Where would you love to go on holiday?

Somewhere hot and chilled out in the middle of nowhere.

If you could be anywhere relaxing right now, where would you be and who would you be with?

A friend of mine has got a villa in the south of Spain with a private pool and everything, and we all went there recently. I only went for two days but I had the best time. I just totally got away from everything. I'd love to be there again. I surprised myself by how chilled out I was.

lee

How do you relax?

By going into the studio. I don't like being at home because I can't relax, I need to have something to take my mind off things. I can't just sit around and chill because I get bored.

Do you play golf/go fishing, etc?

Nah, it's not my thing.

What was the last...

Book you read?

Antony bought me Ozzy Ozbourne's book so I'm trying to get through that at the moment. I really want to read it because Ant bought it for me and it's the first book anyone's ever bought me. I think Ant is trying to encourage me to read.

Film you watched?

Detox with Sylvester Stallone. I watched it with Simon.

CD you listened to?

Brian McKnight, Anytime.

TV programme you watched?

Eastenders.

What's your all-time favourite…

Film?
Stand By Me.

Book?
The Basketball Diaries. It's the only book I've read.

TV show?
Only Fools and Horses.

Album?
Babyface, Live in New York.

Who do you like to chill out with?
I like to be on my own with my thoughts.

How do you totally de-stress?
I sit in the studio. I find it hard to wind down and I like being on the go, so I like being in the studio for hours, just sitting there. I feel content there because I can just chill and write lyrics and express what I'm feeling at that time. I know it sounds weird, but that's what helps me. It's like my therapy.

Are you into therapies, like massage?
Yeah, everyone likes massage!

How much sleep do you need?

I can survive on three hours. I've got so much energy.

What position do you sleep in?

I lie on my front with my head to the side, which is apparently really bad for your back because you're twisting your head to the side so your back is in an 'S' shape.

Where is your favourite place to escape to?

The studio, every time.

Where is your favourite holiday destination?

Scotland. I went there last Christmas and I had a wicked time. The scenery was absolutely beautiful.

Where would you love to go on holiday?

A couple of universes away. I'd like to go to a different planet where's there's life like us and see what's happening.

If you could be anywhere relaxing right now, where would you be and who would you be with?

I'd be with my mates on holiday, having a laugh and chilling.

boys in blue

Antony, Duncan, Simon and Lee have done more in their short time together than most bands do in their entire career. Here they talk about the highlights, the future, and why their friendship will always be the most important thing to them.

What's been the most amazing thing to happen to you since you've been in Blue?

Lee:

I appreciate everything we've achieved, like the awards and shows we've performed at.
It's been amazing so far.

Antony:

There have been so many. Some of the highlights were winning Best Newcomer award at the
BRIT Awards, and another was the Party At The Palace.

Simon:

I think that was the highlight for me. We've met Prince Charles a couple of times now.

Antony:

It was amazing because the first time we met him we were talking to him about warming up our
voices and stuff, and the second time we met him he remembered the conversation. I was well
impressed with that.

Simon:

It's nice to know that he was actually listening to us.

Antony:

William and Harry told us they wish we'd been on more during the concert instead of some of
the other performers, because they really like our music… That was cool.

Duncan:

It was amazing performing alongside people like Paul McCartney. It's probably the last time
there will be such a big event where you get all these big artists together in one place.

What has shocked you about being in the band?

Simon:

Just the success we've had so early on. We've still got so much we want to do around Europe and America, but our rise to fame has been so quick. In the beginning I could get on buses and tubes and no-one would notice me, then all of a sudden I couldn't walk down the street without being recognised.

Antony:

I've been shocked by how many 'pretend' people there are in the business. I did work experience at LWT when I was 16 and the cameramen gave me a really hard time, then when we released All Rise I saw them and they were all really nice to me just because I was on the other side. Things like that do my head in. I hate falseness.

Lee:

It's amazing how many people talk crap. I chat to them and it spins me out. It's also weird how people perceive you. It's like they've already made their mind up what you're like before you've even talked to them. Then when they do talk to you they're trying to suss you out all the time. It's weird. I don't know how anyone can ever get used to this business. It's a crazy place.

Duncan:

It shocked me how people change towards you. Some people look at you differently, and you know that they're waiting for you to change. I think a lot of the time it's not you who changes, it's the people around you. People can treat you differently just because they've seen you on TV. It really shocks me how people put you up high, and then call you arrogant because you're not trying to be their best friend. I don't know them so why would I want to be their best mate? I wouldn't be if I wasn't famous, so I don't have to be their mate just because I'm in a band. People judge you very quickly, which is weird because I would never judge them.

What about being in a band is like you expected it to be, and what isn't?

Lee:

Some of it is like I expected it to be, but a lot of it isn't. I thought I'd be doing a lot more singing, but a lot of it is doing shoots and interviews and going on TV shows. I didn't expect to be doing so much of that.

Duncan:

It's more controlled than I thought it would be. I knew it was going to be a business and we would be a product, but I wasn't prepared for the fakeness that exists. I didn't realise it could sometimes be so shallow. I wasn't ready for cattiness and the backstabbing. I didn't know what to expect.

Simon:

I think our friendship is how I expected it to be, though. We're four guys who genuinely like each other, and it's not like we're struggling to get on with each other every day. We deal with all our problems and it's all pretty laid back.

Antony:

I agree with Si, I always knew we'd get on. I could never go to work knowing I didn't get on with these guys. I love the boys, and we're having a laugh and not taking ourselves too seriously.

What have you learnt about each other?

Simon:

Nothing really, we knew each other really well already.

Antony:

We knew all each other's bad habits and stuff. Personally I wouldn't share a room with Lee or Dunk because they're not exactly tidy, and they're usually up until four in the morning talking, and I need my sleep. And they're so unorganised. But I already knew all that!

Lee:

I think we understand each other really well. We know what to expect from each other because we spend a lot of time together.

Duncan:

We've learnt that the most important thing for us is our friendship, as long as we can rely on each other that's what matters.

What would you change about your time in Blue?

Lee:

I don't think I'd change anything because I don't dwell on the past. But I wish some people would stop saying that we've changed because I don't think we have. I'm the same person I've always been. We all are. But those people can believe what they want.

Duncan:

I would be a bit more chilled out sometimes and not get so het up about little things. Things get escalated out of all proportion, but at the end of the day they don't matter. If I could change me, I think I would be less paranoid of the industry. I wouldn't get myself so worked up and worried about stuff.

Antony:

I'd change my hairstyles. I also hated our styling before we started working with Caroline, our stylist. I can't watch the All Rise video because I think we look terrible.

Simon:

I look at Lee in that video and he looks about ten.

Antony:

I wish I could rewind and take pictures of us and everything we've done. I really regret not doing that because we can't look back on everything that easily.

Simon:

I wish someone had had a camera on us 24 hours a day because we've got our memories, but you can't always get things across to people.

What would you love the band to achieve?

Simon:

I think we just want to carry on the way we are. We're loving it.

Duncan:

We just want continued success. As long as we continue to be healthy and make good music and people continue to love it, we're happy.

What bands have you made friends with?

Simon:

Bands that we're genuinely friends with are Sugababes, Damage, Westlife, Mis-teeq, Liberty X and 3SL.

Antony:

We don't not get on with anyone, but some solo artists are quite closed off. I'm not too bothered though. If they don't want to chat, that's fine.

Have you made any faux pas since you've been in Blue, like falling over on stage, etc?

Simon:

I nearly fell off stage yesterday. I nearly fell over some camera wires. The cameraman was right in my face.

Antony:

I nearly crashed into a cameraman the other day. They get up so close to you.

Lee:

I think it's funny when stuff like that happens! I don't mind it when I make mistakes.

Duncan:

But we've all been pretty lucky, touch wood. We haven't had anything too bad happen.

What's your biggest row in the band been about?

Antony:

We don't row, we just have the odd petty argument about dance routines and what we're going to sing. It's always stuff to do with the job. It's not like we fall out because someone has got a better hairstyle than someone else.

Duncan:

The only time we argue is if someone is a bit tired or ratty, but we know when to leave each other alone.

What's been the biggest compliment you've ever had about the band?

Antony:

That people like our music. That means the most to us. People like Mis-teeq and Liberty X will tell us they like our music, and it's nice that other artists like what you're doing.

Lee:

I like it when people say that we're different and we're not like a boy band. People have compared us to Backstreet boys which is wicked because they can all really sing. Compliments are brilliant, but we try not to let them go to our heads.

Duncan:

I like it when people say that we're nice guys and we've got a good American sound, and that we'd do really well in America. But the best thing is that people say we're genuine. We have our days when we're a bit grumpy and run down. You can't be shiny happy people 24/7, but we are ourselves. A lot of people you meet expect you to be smiley all the time, but we're just us and we don't have any airs and graces or look down on anyone. We are who we are. We come from a good background and we've been brought up well by our parents.

How long do you think Blue will be around?

Simon:

As long as people want us around.

Antony:

We know it's not going to last for years and years because other pop bands will be coming up. We'd love it to last for years and years, but I think boys bands generally last about four or five years. When people stop recognising us in the street then we'll stop.

Lee:

We'll keep on going until we've had enough. I love the second album and I feel like we're progressing. As long as people still want to listen to our music, and as long as we're still getting on, we'll carry on. But I think our friendship is more important than the band because it will be around long after the band is.

Duncan:

We want the future to be fun, and we want to be happy. You can be happy being a dustman or a pop star, it doesn't matter. I want us to be happy first and foremost. We've all got a lot of ambitions and aspirations that go beyond Blue, and we're all determined to do other stuff after Blue. But you can't have a better start than Blue, and I think that if we all keep on the way we are, all of our careers can go through the roof.

How do you see the future?

Simon:

Bright and blue!

AWARDS

Pepsi Chart – **Best Newcomer**

2001 Smash Hits – **Poll Winners Best Newcomer 2001**

Capital 95.8 Award – **London's Favourite Newcomer 2001**

Capital 95.8 Award – **London's Favourite Single 2001 (If You Come Back)**

Capital 95.8 Award – **London's Best Pop Act 2001** as voted for by readers of 'News Of The World'

Brit Award – **Best British Newcomer 2001**

Nordorf Robbins Award – **Best New Artist 2001**

The Sun – **Best Newcomer Award 2001**

PICTURE CREDITS

With special thanks to Francis Loney and Jasper for the original photography throughout.

Our thanks also to the following contributors: **Rex Features, Famous, PA Photos**

P9   Brit Awards, February 2002, Best British Newcomer **(Brian Rasic/Rex Features)**

P21   Blue on-stage at Party in the Park, July 2002 **(Yui Mok/PA Photos)**

P21   Duncan on-stage at Party in the Park, July 2002 **(Yui Mok/PA Photos)**

P40   Launch of 'Too Close', HMV Oxford Street, August 2001 **(Yui Mok/PA Photos)**

P48   Motown performance, Queen's Golden Jubilee 'Party at the Palace', June 2002
        (Tim Rooke/Rex Features)

P51   Antony **(Roger Woolman/Famous)**

P51   Duncan **(Hugo Correira/Famous)**

P54   Simon **(Roger Woolman/Famous)**

P54   Lee **(Roger Woolman/Famous)**

P66   Vienna, Austria, March 2002 **(Karl Schoendorfer/Rex Features)**

P68   Signing autographs at the Capital Radio Awards, March 2002
        (Nils Jorgesen/Rex Features)

P82   Winners at the Capital Radio Awards, March 2002 **(Richard Young/Rex Features)**

P83   Launching 02 mobile phones at the London Eye, May 2002 **(Brian Rasic/Rex Features)**

P140   Backstage at the Queen's Golden Jubilee 'Party at the Palace', June 2002
        (Peter Jordan/PA Photos)

P142   Capital Radio Awards, March 2002 **(Tim Rooke/Rex Features)**

P150   Performing with Tom Jones, Queen's Golden Jubilee 'Party at the Palace', June 2002
        (Tim Rooke/Rex Features)

P154   With Ant and Dec, National Television Awards 2001 **(Richard Young/Rex Features)**

blueonblue